A Pictorial History
of the
Northern
Mariana Islands
Part II
The Japanese Era

Written and illustrated by
Beverly Battaglia

AuthorHouse™ LLC
1663 Liberty Drive
Bloomington, IN 47403
www.authorhouse.com
Phone: 1-800-839-8640

Published by AuthorHouse   06/05/2014

ISBN: 978-1-4918-1609-7 (sc)
ISBN: 978-1-4918-1610-3 (e)

Also by Beverly Battaglia:
A Pictorial History of the Northern Mariana Islands, Part 1

Library of Congress Control Number: 2013916429

This book is printed on acid-free paper.

Table of Contents

INTRODUCTION

If you have already read *A Pictorial History of the Northern Mariana Islands, Part I –*

feel free to skip the next five pages.

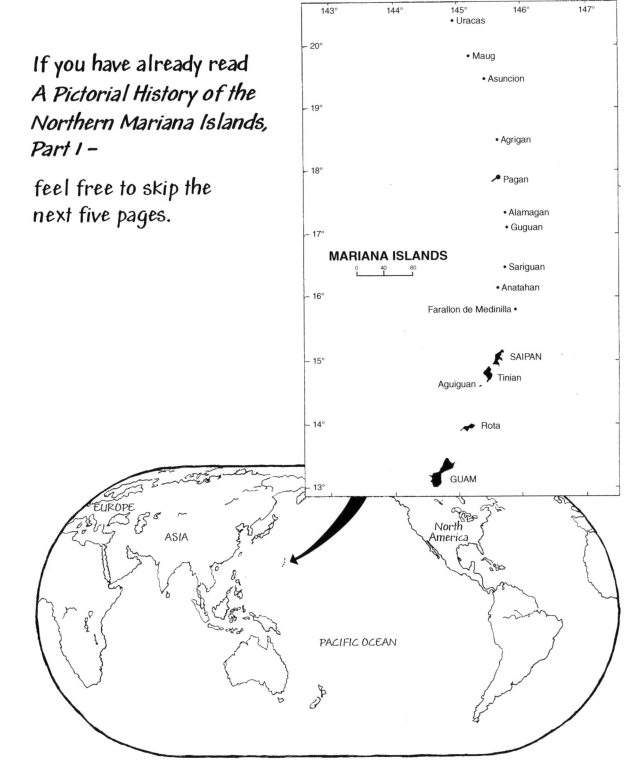

Once upon a time, there were these beautiful Micronesian Islands in the middle of the Pacific Ocean ...

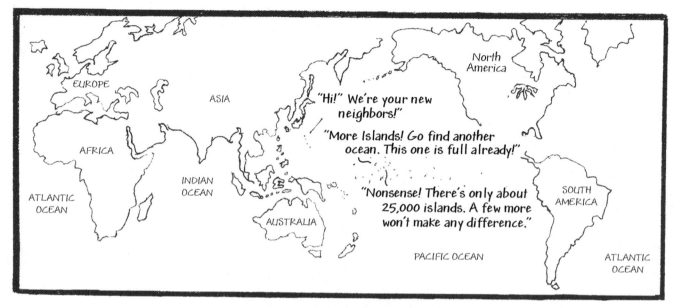

ISLAND FORMATION
about 52 million years ago

These islands were eventually called the Mariana Islands. They were inhabited by people who called themselves "Chamorros."

CHAMORRO SETTLEMENT
about 1500 B.C.

The Chamorros wore only hats and shoes. They fished, farmed and lived in houses built on top of pillars called latte stones.

ANCIENT CHAMORROS
1500 BC — 1521 AD

Ferdinand Magellan arrived at the islands in 1521 during his famous voyage that circumnavigated the world ...

EUROPEAN DISCOVERY
1521 AD

In 1668, Father Diego Luis Sanvitores arrived on Guam with some missionaries to bring Christianity to the Chamorros.

REDUCCIÓN
1668-1698

By 1698, all the Chamorros had been converted to Christianity. In the process of achieving this conversion, many Chamorros died. The Spanish moved the surviving Chamorros off the northern islands, forcing them all to live on Guam or Rota.

SPANISH ADMINISTRATION
1698-1898

Around 1810 some natives from the Caroline Islands moved north to live on Saipan.

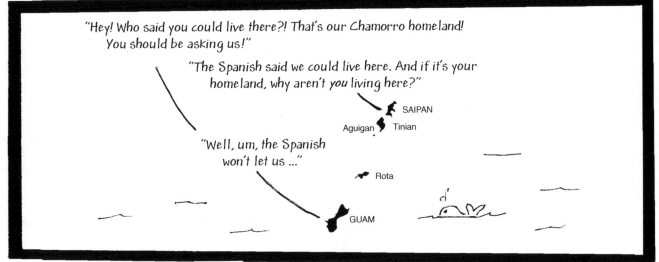

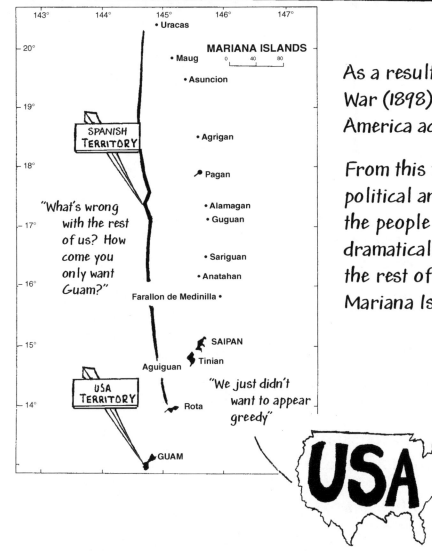

As a result of the Spanish American War (1898), the United States of America acquired the island of Guam.

From this time forward, personal, political and social experiences of the people living on Guam were dramatically different from those of the rest of the islands—the Northern Mariana Islands.

In 1899, Spain sold her remaining island possessions in Micronesia, including the Northern Mariana Islands, to Germany.

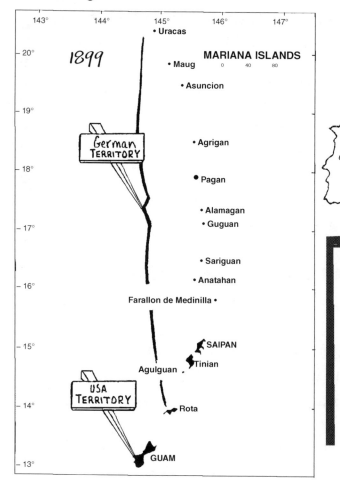

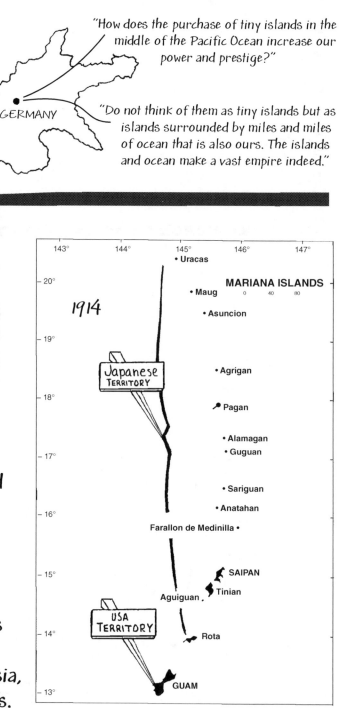

"How does the purchase of tiny islands in the middle of the Pacific Ocean increase our power and prestige?"

"Do not think of them as tiny islands but as islands surrounded by miles and miles of ocean that is also ours. The islands and ocean make a vast empire indeed."

On August 9, 1914, Japan entered World War I on the side of the Allies (Great Britain, France, and later, the United States) against the Central Powers (Germany, Austria and Turkey).

In the same year Japan sent battleships Eastward and proceeded to capture all the German-owned islands in Micronesia, including the Northern Mariana Islands.

The ownership of the Northern Mariana Islands changed hands 3 times in 21 years.

And now,
this story continues ...

World War I
1914-1918

Not much fighting occurred when the Northern Mariana Islands changed hands during World War I. The Japanese moved into and took over the German-held islands without a shot being fired. Overnight, the authority changed; German officials were shipped out. The Chamorros and Carolinians answered to a new foreign power.

Capturing islands in the Pacific provided no military advantage to further the Allied cause in World War I. Obtaining these lands, however, did provide a strategic advantage for Japan. Japan was a rising industrial power seeking raw materials and an outlet for goods it produced. The islands also increased Japanese land holdings and provided a buffer zone for military defense.

The War Years
1914–1918

While the rest of the world waged War, the Japanese waged peace.

In 1915, the Japanese government sent men to survey the Northern Mariana Islands to determine their economic potential.

"I was just talking to that nice Japanese gentleman. He wanted to know all about the best farmlands, what we grow, where the wells are ..."

"Why all the questions?"

"He said he was just curious."

"Sure—I wonder what he's up to?"

"What do you mean?"

"You surely don't think the capture of our islands had any real strategic importance to a war fought primarily in Europe, do you?"

"True ..."

"So, why'd they capture us?"

"Good point. I wonder what he's up to?"

It set up schools to teach Japanese language and customs.

"Why do I have to go to school, Mom?"

"So, you can learn to speak Japanese."

"But I already speak Chamorro, Carolinian, Spanish, and German. Isn't that enough?"

"Apparently not."

Kogakko

A kogakko was a public school for Micronesian children

The Japanese government provided free health care and medical treatment.

"Did you hear—the Japanese are providing health care for free! Isn't that great! They must really care a lot about us."

"That or they just don't want to catch whatever we've got."

HOSPITAL

On July 1, 1918, a Civil Affairs Bureau was created where Japanese civilians would administer the government of the islands instead of naval officers. July 1 was celebrated as "Foundation Day."

"It says here we're getting a civilian government. What happened to the military? Is the war over?"

"No. They're all still fighting."

"But—a civilian government is like what Japan has with its territories. Have we become a Japanese Territory?"

"It would seem so."

"Can they do that? Turn us into Japanese property with the stroke of a pen?"

"Who's to stop them?"

"But—what happens to us if the Germans win?"

"Good question."

8

Japanese Mandate
1920-1935

In 1853, United States Navy Commodore Matthew C. Perry forced the Japanese government to open its doors to Western trade. Afterwards, the Japanese government started a policy of modernization and expansion. Acquisition of more islands in the Pacific Ocean fit in with this policy.

Present since 1914, Japan retained its control of the Northern Mariana Islands after World War I ended. In theory, determining the future of the islands was a responsibility of the newly formed League of Nations.

The League of Nations designated the indigenous residents of the Pacific Islands as "not ready for self-government." This meant the responsibility for their development and growth would be placed under a sponsoring government.

In 1920 the League of Nations granted official control of the Pacific islands, including the Northern Mariana Islands, to Japan under vicarious authority calling it a "mandate."

Japanese Sugar Train

Japanese Expansion
Land Acquisitions: 1862 — 1935

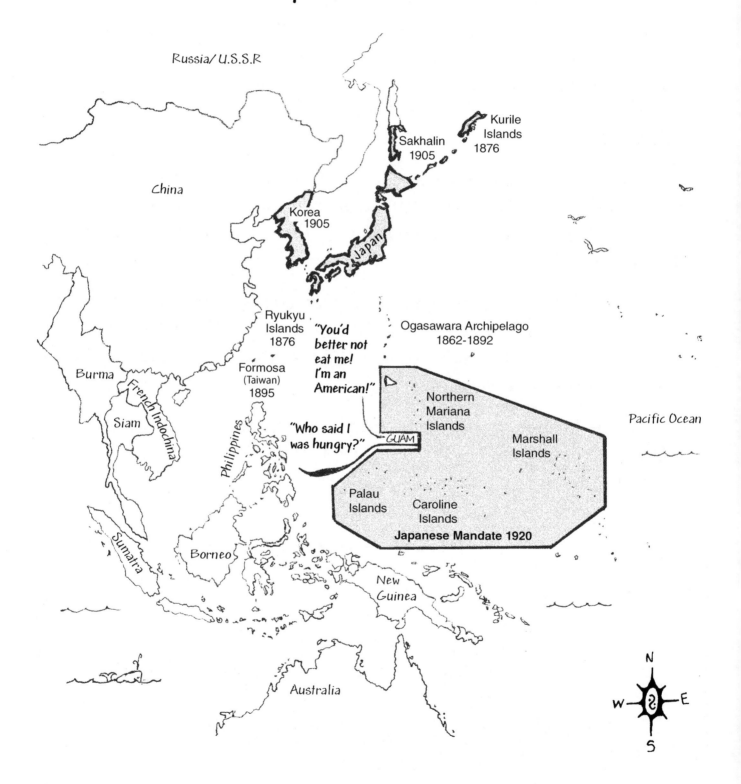

Events Around the World
1920-1935

Europe
1920's

Genocide-Greek and Assyrian
Greco Turkish war
Russian Revolution
Price riots in Germany
Joseph Stalin becomes Secretary General of the Soviet Union
Benito Mussolini becomes Dictator of Italy
Stalin begins purge of rivals
Hyperinflation in Germany
Major earthquakes in Greece, Yugoslavia, and Bulgaria

1930-35

Italians occupy Libya
Bloody Sunday in Germany
Famine in the Ukraine
Adolph Hitler becomes Chancellor of Germany
Nazi Party takes power in Germany/Jews persecuted
Italians invade Ethiopia

Asia
1920's

Soviet army captures Mongolia
Great Kanto earthquake in Japan
Shanghai Massacre in China
Chinese Civil War
Japanese banking crisis
Major earthquakes in Japan and China
Japanese troops move into China (Jinan incident)
Hirohito becomes Emperor of Japan

1930-35

Major earthquakes in China and Japan
Floods in China
Japan occupies Shanghai
Severe economic depression in Japan
Earthquake and tsunami in Japan
Massive crop failures in Japan

North America (USA)
1920's

Prohibition begins
Tulsa race riots (Oklahoma)
Red scare
Teapot Dome Scandal
Mississippi River floods
Hurricane in Miami (Florida)
Tornado in St. Louis (Missouri)
San Francisco dam breaks (Calif.)
St. Valentine Day's Massacre (Illinois)
Stock Market crash—Wall Street crisis
The Great Depression begins

1930-35

Depression continues-14 million unemployed
World War I Veteran's Bonus March
Franklin D. Roosevelt becomes U.S. President
Dust storms begin in the Midwest
Dustbowl begins forcing families to move west

EUROPE

ASIA

Northern Mariana Islands
1920-1935
Economic boom
Sugar production

North America

"Mom, I want to travel and see the world ..."
"I think you might want to wait a while first ..."

A Closer Look at the Mandate

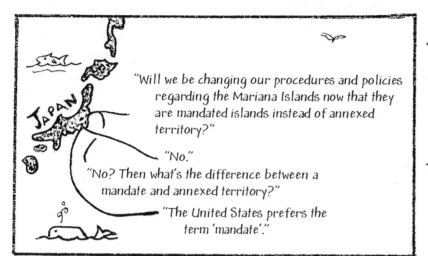

"Will we be changing our procedures and policies regarding the Mariana Islands now that they are mandated islands instead of annexed territory?"

"No."

"No? Then what's the difference between a mandate and annexed territory?"

"The United States prefers the term 'mandate'."

Japan originally planned to annex the lands it acquired during World War I. The United States objected fearing an annexation would give Japan too much military power in the Pacific.

The League of Nations proposed the Mandate System as a compromise. Japan would govern, but not own the islands.

The League of Nations determined that the people of Mandated Territories were those ...

...not yet able to stand by themselves under the strenuous conditions of the modern world.

"It says we're a 'mandate.' What's a 'mandate'?"

"A mandate is a commission to act for another. In this case, the Japanese have been commissioned to act for us."

"But why? I can take care of myself."

"Tell that to the Japanese."

"I would, but they've got too many guns."

"Hi. I'm here to survey this land for the Japanese government. Now, who owns this?"

"Um, no one, really. We all share it and use it together."

"No one owns the land. I'll just mark it down as government property."

"What does that mean?"

"Not much. You'll just have to pay a fee to the government to use it from now on."

"I think the Japanese need to reread the mandate objectives."

The mandate charter states that the Mandatory (Japanese Emperor) shall ...

... promote to the utmost the material and moral well-being ... of the inhabitants ...

Japan pledged not to use the Mandated Islands for military or naval purposes. (Article 4, Mandate Charter)

"How can we confirm Japan hasn't built any fortifications in the Mandated Islands?"

"Look and see for ourselves."

"But what if Japan refuses us entry to look?"

"Well, I guess that would be a good indication that the Japanese are building something ..."

American Flag

"Why are foreigners refused entry into the Mandated Islands?"

"Well, we can't build fortifications there so secrecy is our only defense. Foreign spies could make maps of the islands and use them to develop attack plans Also, we need no outside comments or criticism concerning how we manage the islands."

"Won't other countries get suspicious if we deny them access?"

"Why? It's not like we're trying to build fortifications or anything."

Japanese Flag

Japan formed the Nanyo-cho, the South Seas Government (or South Seas Bureau) in 1922. Its headquarters was located on Palau. The Nanyo-choan (governor) reported directly to the Prime Minister of Japan.

Japanese Administrators were professionals and their selection was based on merit, not politics. Graft and/or corruption was rare during the Japanese Administration of the Mandated Islands.

"Thanks for your help. You're really good. Whatever did you do wrong to get yourself posted here?"

"What do you mean? I requested it."

"Really? But surely you must be a relative of an important official to get your request ..."

"No."

"I don't understand ..."

"Well, I studied, trained, and got this job because I am the best."

"You mean to say you're not being punished? You're not related to anyone and you got this job because you've good at it?"

"That's right."

"Employing people because they're qualified! What a strange idea! I like it, but it's strange."

Japanese Office

Haruji Matsue

In 1920, Haruji Matsue visited the Northern Mariana Islands. He decided sugarcane could be successfully grown there. To this end he gained support from the Japanese government and put his plan in action.

In 1921, Mr. Matsue acquired all available land leases. Then he brought in poor Okinawan tenant farmers to raise sugarcane. He built a sugarcane factory and railroad tracks. He brought in a train to carry the sugarcane to the factory for processing.

Mr. Matsue's efforts at sugarcane production were highly successful. He turned the quiet Northern Mariana Islands into a booming economy.

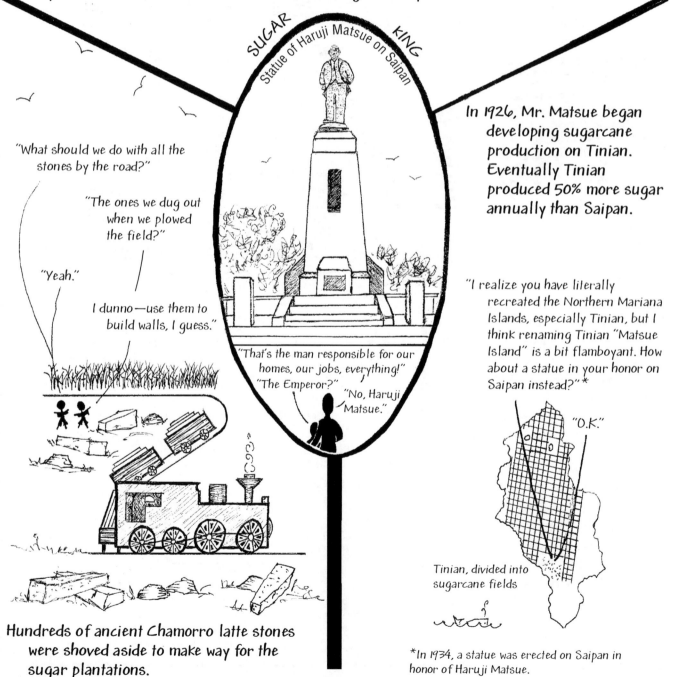

SUGAR KING

Statue of Haruji Matsue on Saipan

"What should we do with all the stones by the road?"

"The ones we dug out when we plowed the field?"

"Yeah."

"I dunno—use them to build walls, I guess."

"That's the man responsible for our homes, our jobs, everything!"
"The Emperor?"
"No, Haruji Matsue."

In 1926, Mr. Matsue began developing sugarcane production on Tinian. Eventually Tinian produced 50% more sugar annually than Saipan.

"I realize you have literally recreated the Northern Mariana Islands, especially Tinian, but I think renaming Tinian "Matsue Island" is a bit flamboyant. How about a statue in your honor on Saipan instead?"*

"O.K."

Tinian, divided into sugarcane fields

Hundreds of ancient Chamorro latte stones were shoved aside to make way for the sugar plantations.

*In 1934, a statue was erected on Saipan in honor of Haruji Matsue.

14

Population Explosion

The large number of Japanese and Koreans imported to work with sugar production resulted in a rapid population increase within the Northern Mariana Islands. The Chamorros and Carolinians were soon outnumbered.

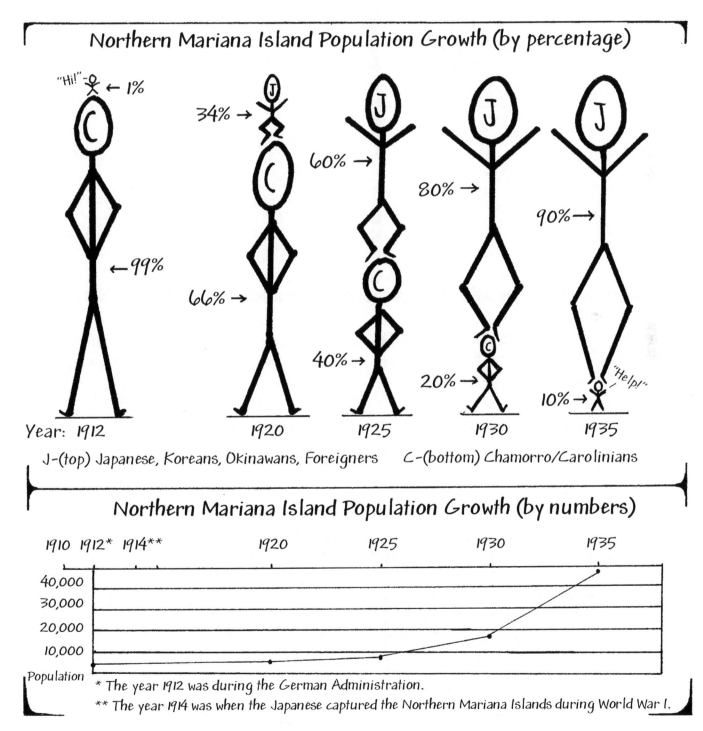

Northern Mariana Island Population Growth (by percentage)

"Hi!" ← 1%
34% →
60% →
80% →
90% →
←99%
66% →
40% →
20% →
10% → "Help!"

Year: 1912   1920   1925   1930   1935

J-(top) Japanese, Koreans, Okinawans, Foreigners   C-(bottom) Chamorro/Carolinians

Northern Mariana Island Population Growth (by numbers)

1910 1912* 1914**   1920   1925   1930   1935

40,000
30,000
20,000
10,000
Population

* The year 1912 was during the German Administration.

** The year 1914 was when the Japanese captured the Northern Mariana Islands during World War I.

Development of the island of Rota began in 1930. Sugarcane was planted. A factory and railroad were built.

Songsong village was modernized. Phosphate deposits were discovered and then mined.

To make room for more Japanese immigrants all the Micronesian residents of Songsong, Rota, were rounded up and forced to move to Tatacho village. Micronesian farmers throughout Rota were forced to move; their traditional farmlands were turned into sugarcane fields.

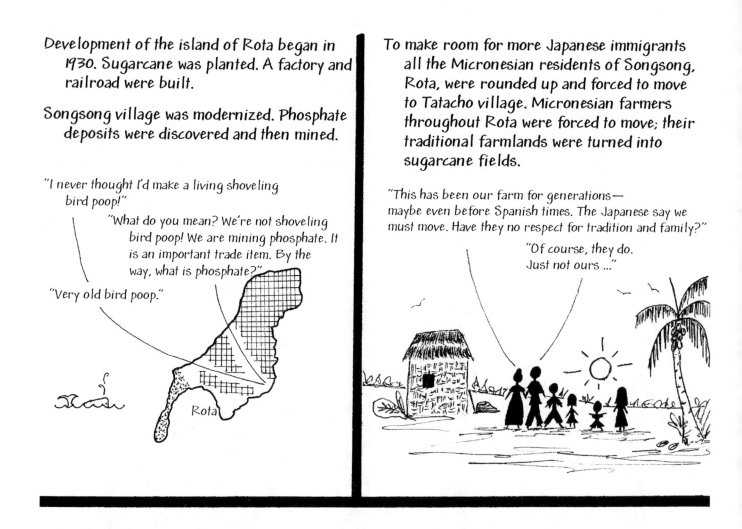

"I never thought I'd make a living shoveling bird poop!"

"What do you mean? We're not shoveling bird poop! We are mining phosphate. It is an important trade item. By the way, what is phosphate?"

"Very old bird poop."

Rota

"This has been our farm for generations— maybe even before Spanish times. The Japanese say we must move. Have they no respect for tradition and family?"

"Of course, they do. Just not ours ..."

Residents in the Northern Mariana Islands lived under a class system with the best positions and treatment reserved for the Japanese citizens. Next came the Okinawans/Koreans and finally, the Chamorros/Carolinians.

"Doesn't it bother you that all the best jobs and foods go to the Japanese?"

"A bit. But then I look around—paved roads, electric lights, telephones, movies, automobiles, trains, doctors, a huge variety of food ... I have more now as a 3rd class Japanese subject than I ever had before!"

The Tachinid Fly

The sugarcane beetle borer damaged most of the first sugarcane crops (1922-23). To eradicate this insect, Matsue had all the cane fields burned and imported the tachinid fly to destroy the cane borer. Thanks to the fly, Matsue was able to export larger and larger amounts of sugar every year.

The tachinid fly was treated with reverence amongst the sugarcane folk.

HERO!
Savior of the Sugar Cane

Tachinid FLY

Microceromasia Sphenophorus vi11

Attracted by the sweet smell of pressed and crushed sugarcane, flies swarmed everywhere sugar was produced.

"Wait! Stop! What are you doing!!"

"I'm getting rid of some flies! They're everywhere and into everything!"

"You can't do that! They might be the good flies—the ones that kill the sugarcane beetle!"

"How do you tell them apart?"

"You can't."

"You mean we're stuck with all the flies?"

" 'Fraid so ..."

While visiting Saipan, author Willard Price reported:

Our Japanese policeman ordered bean soup. When it was set before him, it contained six flies. We watched with curiosity. Would he send it back? Would he pick out the flies with his chopsticks?

He raised the bowl to his mouth, locked his long upper teeth over the edge to form a sieve, and drank the soup. The six flies remained in the bowl.

He smiled. "We get used to them," he said.

Island Pests

Other visitors came to the Northern Mariana Islands during the Japanese Administration of the Mandated Islands. Their descendants can still be found on the islands.

"What is it?"

"It's a cane toad."

"Can you eat it?"

"No. It's poisonous."

"What's it for?"

"It's supposed to eat bugs in the sugarcane fields, but it doesn't."

"So are the Japanese going to take them back?"

"Can't—there's too many of them!"

"So ... we're stuck?"

"Looks like it."

The Japanese imported the Bufo Marinas, or cane toad, to eat the beetles in the sugarcane fields.

Unfortunately, the beetles only came out in the daytime to eat, and the toad only came out at night to feed, so the two never met.

The great African snail first appeared during the Japanese Administration. Lacking a natural predator, the snails multiplied quickly destroying gardens and vegetation throughout the islands.

"Look what I found in the garden! They're everywhere!"

"Yeah. They're in my garden too!"

"They're eating all my plants! What can I do?"

"Um, I've heard you can eat them ... "

"—?!— You first."

"Ow! That's the fifth bee sting today! We never had these bees before. You think the Japanese brought them in just to keep us out of the jungle?"

"Naw—I saw some of these bees in the Chinese cargo last week. Maybe they should inspect the cargo better in case something really undesirable tries to come ashore ..."

"Like what?"

"I don't know, maybe a snake ..."

The yellow oriental paper wasp (also referred to as a boonie bee) comes from Asia. It was most likely introduced in the Northern Mariana Islands during the Japanese Administration.

This wasp is very fast and very territorial. It will attack anyone that jostles or threatens its nest.

Meanwhile...

While many things changed with the arrival of the Japanese, some things did not:

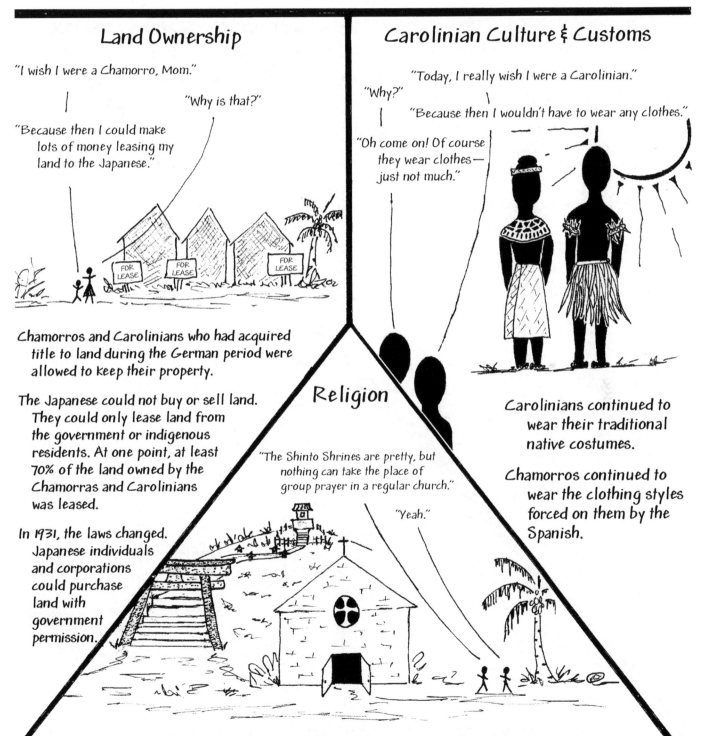

Land Ownership

"I wish I were a Chamorro, Mom."

"Why is that?"

"Because then I could make lots of money leasing my land to the Japanese."

Chamorros and Carolinians who had acquired title to land during the German period were allowed to keep their property.

The Japanese could not buy or sell land. They could only lease land from the government or indigenous residents. At one point, at least 70% of the land owned by the Chamorras and Carolinians was leased.

In 1931, the laws changed. Japanese individuals and corporations could purchase land with government permission.

Carolinian Culture & Customs

"Today, I really wish I were a Carolinian."

"Why?"

"Because then I wouldn't have to wear any clothes."

"Oh come on! Of course they wear clothes — just not much."

Carolinians continued to wear their traditional native costumes.

Chamorros continued to wear the clothing styles forced on them by the Spanish.

Religion

"The Shinto Shrines are pretty, but nothing can take the place of group prayer in a regular church."

"Yeah."

Chamorros and Carolinians were encouraged to participate in the national Japanese religion, Shintoism, but few adopted it.

Surahana/Surahanu

The Surahana (female)/Surahanu (male) is a Chamorro Healer. They use native plants and traditional methods to heal patients. Many of their remedies could date back to ancient Chamorro times (before 1521 AD).

During the Reducción (1668-1681) the Spanish forbade all practices that appeared non-Christian in nature. Somehow the healing crafts of the Surahana/u managed to survive this purge.

"The Priests are forbidding everything they don't like! What if they forbid us to heal? Our people will die if we can't heal. What'll we do?"

"Maybe we can add prayer to our healing."

"Prayer?"

"You know, special words like the Priests says in Church."

"Those are just meaningless sounds."

"I know, but the Priests think those sounds are important. Who knows, maybe they can help. At the very least, including prayer might make the Priests happy enough to let us continue healing."

"I hope so."

1680

"I don't feel so good."

"Did you see the doctor?"

"I tried, but the line was so long . . . Besides, it's hard to find the right words in Japanese to describe my problem ..."

"Why don't you see the Surahana?"

"Good idea. I think I will."

1930

Despite the arrival of modern medicine and medical procedures, Surahanas and Surahanus have continued to practice their craft and still heal people in the Mariana Islands.

A Taga House Story

Built between 1400–1500 AD supposedly by Chief Taga, the greatest of all ancient Chamorros, Taga House has the largest standing latte stones in the Marianas. The Japanese cleared away hundreds of latte stones to make way for sugar plantations, but not Taga House. The reason why was told to the author by an elderly Chamorro gentleman ...

"Hey! What are you doing!"

"We're clearing away these old stones so we can put up some more shops."

"You can't do that! These stones are sacred. It's bad luck to disturb them."

"Nonsense. They're just a bunch of rocks."

One day the Japanese decided they needed more space in Tinian Town and decided to tear down and haul away the huge stones of Taga House. ...

"Where is everyone?"

"The workers got sick last night."

"Maybe it *is* unlucky to move the stones ..."

They had barely begun when workers mysteriously became ill; the equipment broke; all sorts of things happened that delayed their efforts ...

"It looks like the Japanese will definitely not be moving Taga House now."

"Great. Now we can stop drugging the worker's food and they'll get well again."

Fearing they had offended some ancient Chamorro spirits, the Japanese stopped removal efforts. They asked a Chamorro Surahana to help them make apologies. The Surahana said special prayers and the Japanese carved and dedicated 2 small latte stones to the site.

Afterwards, the workers got well. The Japanese never again tried to move the stones of Taga House.

"Amazing!"

"What? That the ancient Chamorros were able to carve out and lift these stones without the help of metal tools or modern machinery?"

"Or that these stones have withstood the ravages of time and still stand here after over 400 years?"

"Actually, I just thought they were really, really big stones ..."

"That, too."

Today

Visitors to Taga House walk between 2 small latte stones on their way to view the final standing latte stones of Taga House.

The rest of the stones at Taga House have fallen. They lay where they first fell—except one capstone (tasi). It can be found across the street from Taga House.

In 1990, that single capstone lay in the jungle almost a mile away from Taga House. No doubt it was moved and left in the jungle by the Japanese many years ago ...

21

Japanese Discipline

The Japanese insisted on strict obedience in all matters.

"Look at you! You're bald! What happened to your hair?"

"I forgot to bow towards Japan before entering the Church."

"You're lucky. Last week a policeman didn't think Jose was being properly respectful so the policeman made him look at the sun ... Jose still can't see properly."

Failure to obey the rules had a variety of consequences including: a beating with a rubber strap or a thick rope; hoisting a person upside down and beating him on the feet; being forced to stare into the sun; being forced to sit on a board put behind the knees; forced to lift a biscuit tin filled with water for half a day; and execution.

Punishments designed to shame an individual included shaving a person's head and forcing people to go naked in public.

"Fritz! You're a mess! There's blood everywhere! What happened? You look like you've been in a fight! Who did this to you?"

"My teacher. I gave the wrong answer to a question in class."

"Oh. Thank goodness you weren't hurt worse. Go clean up and then get to studying— you don't want this to happen again."

The teacher had absolute power in the classroom. Punishment was often physically violent. Students who misbehaved or did not perform to expectations might be beaten, slapped repeatedly on the face, hit with a ruler or leather strap, or beaten on the head until blood ran out of the nose. Other punishments included running laps, shaming by being forced to wear costumes or signs proclaiming one's errors, and group guilt such as punishing the whole class for the errors of a single student. Some students actually died as a result of school punishment.

This & That

The Japanese believed themselves to be racially superior to all others.

"Mother! My teacher says all Americans are barbarians!"

Nonsense, dear. Your uncle Jose on Guam works for the Americans. He wouldn't if they were barbarians, would he?"

"I guess not. But why would my teacher say such things?"

"I don't know—but don't argue with him about it. I don't want you to get in trouble."

Kogakku

Every year the Japanese filed a report with the League of Nations concerning its progress with the Mandate. The commission members who reviewed the reports never once actually visited the Mandated Territory.

"This report really makes the Japanese look good. I wonder how all this economic activity affects the natives?"

"Why don't you go to the Mandate and see for yourself?"

"That would never do. The Japanese might think we don't trust them."

MANDATE COMMISSION

The Japanese offered various jobs throughout Micronesia to Chamorros and Carolinians. Some of the Chamorros and Carolinians who took jobs on other islands decided to remain there permanently.

"Guess what! I just got a job working at a cable station on Yap!"

"Yap! Why there? Yap is so far away! It's primitive, too!"

"I know! I hear the women still go topless there!"

Despite the tropical environment, Japanese settlers persisted in eating traditional foods imported from Japan—canned fish, pickles, miso paste, seaweed and rice.

Breadfruit

Banana

Coconut

"We're Japanese. We eat Japanese food. Why would you want to eat any of the locally produced food?"

mango

YAMS

Sweet Potatoes

Spying in the Marianas

In general, the Japanese government did not permit foreigners to visit the Mandated Islands. Convinced the Japanese were hiding something, officials of the American government continually sought ways to find out what.

In October 1922, Earl H. "Pete" Ellis entered the Mandated Islands to collect information for the Americans. While Ellis may have considered himself a spy, his presence was no secret to the Japanese.

"... Oh, and keep an eye on the American spy ..."

"SPY! There's a spy in the Mandate? How will I know him?"

"Tall, loud, white skin, brown hair, usually drunk ... The only Caucasian on the island. He's hard to miss."

Police Station

Scientists admitted into the Mandated Islands were asked to keep their "eyes and ears open" and report their observations to the American government.

"Inform the Saipan Office that an American spy is on the way ..."

"Spy?!! But I thought he was a scientist. What makes you think he's a spy?"

"Because he was brought here by a United States Navy ship. I doubt the American government provides transportation for mere civilians ..."

Nanyo-Cho
South Seas Government

In 1935, noted author and journalist Willard DeMille Price and his wife Mary took a 4-month tour through the Japanese Mandated Islands. They found gaining entry into the Mandate area most difficult.

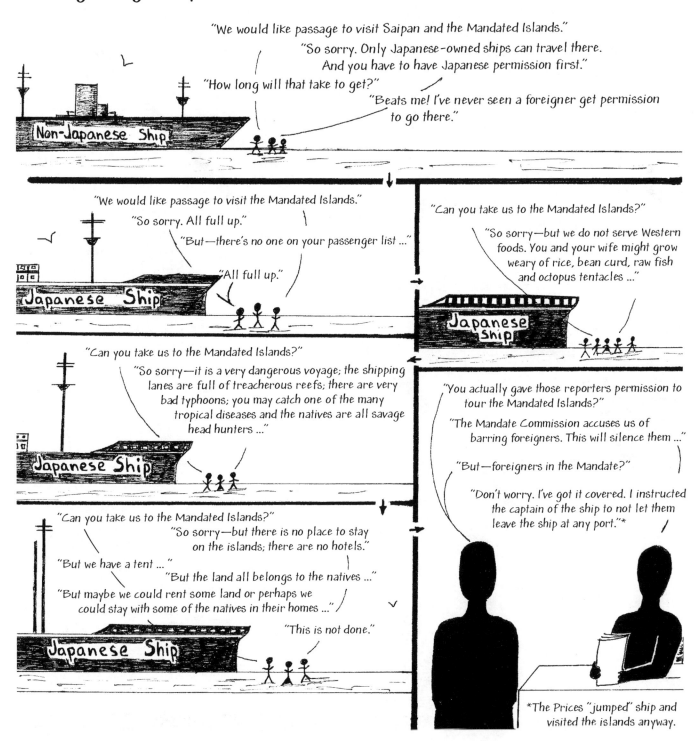

"We would like passage to visit Saipan and the Mandated Islands."

"So sorry. Only Japanese-owned ships can travel there. And you have to have Japanese permission first."

"How long will that take to get?"

"Beats me! I've never seen a foreigner get permission to go there."

Non-Japanese Ship

"We would like passage to visit the Mandated Islands."

"So sorry. All full up."

"But—there's no one on your passenger list ..."

"All full up."

Japanese Ship

"Can you take us to the Mandated Islands?"

"So sorry—but we do not serve Western foods. You and your wife might grow weary of rice, bean curd, raw fish and octopus tentacles ..."

Japanese Ship

"Can you take us to the Mandated Islands?"

"So sorry—it is a very dangerous voyage; the shipping lanes are full of treacherous reefs; there are very bad typhoons; you may catch one of the many tropical diseases and the natives are all savage head hunters ..."

Japanese Ship

"You actually gave those reporters permission to tour the Mandated Islands?"

"The Mandate Commission accuses us of barring foreigners. This will silence them ..."

"But—foreigners in the Mandate?"

"Don't worry. I've got it covered. I instructed the captain of the ship to not let them leave the ship at any port."*

"Can you take us to the Mandated Islands?"

"So sorry—but there is no place to stay on the islands; there are no hotels."

"But we have a tent ... "

"But the land all belongs to the natives ..."

"But maybe we could rent some land or perhaps we could stay with some of the natives in their homes ..."

"This is not done."

Japanese Ship

*The Prices "jumped" ship and visited the islands anyway.

In the 1930's the Japanese relationship with the United States, never that good to begin with, deteriorated further and the Japanese government began to prepare for military conflict.

Construction of potential military facilities was begun, including expanding Tanapag Harbor in Saipan, making it capable of landing amphibious aircraft (completed in 1932) and building Aslito Airfield on Saipan (completed in 1934).

"With our deeper harbor and new airfield we'll be international! We'll have people and materials from around the world!"

"I doubt it."

"What do you mean?"

"Well the harbor's been done for 2 years now and have you seen any foreign ships docking?"

"Well, no —"

"So what makes you think you'll see any foreign planes land?"

"But if it wasn't for more trade, what did they build them for?"

"Good question ..."

All communication to and from Guam was cut off by the Japanese government in 1935.

"Unpack the bags. Our trip is off. No ships are going to Guam."

"We've been planning this trip for months."

"What will Grandma say?"

"Grandma will understand. But when will we see her again?"

"I don't know. The Japanese won't say. You'd think the people on Guam were enemies or something."

26

"What was it like when you were little, Grandma?"

"It was very different from now: Very quiet."

"Quiet? What do you mean?"

"Well, there were only a few of us on the Islands and then we were mostly Chamorros and Carolinians."

"No Japanese?"

"Only a few. And they weren't in charge."

"They didn't give the orders? That's hard to believe. What did they do?"

"I think he ran a store."

"A store? Just one? Who ran the others?"

"Others? There was only one other store and it belonged to the government."

"That's it? Surely there was something else ... "

"There was the Church, and our homes, of course."

"What—No factories? No mines? No refineries? No mills? No markets? No stations? No runways?"

"That's right. And no trains or planes or autos or bikes or movie theaters or clothing stores or candy shops. No Koreans or Okinawans or sugarcane plantations ..."

"But—do you mean there was—nothing?"

"We had a lot of jungle then."

"Weren't you lonely? What did you do?"

"We didn't think we were lonely. We worked; we played; we sang; we prayed. We were always busy."

"Gee—you sure didn't have much. And think of all we have now! Just look at the progress we have made since then. Aren't you glad the Japanese came and brought us all this?"

"I suppose so. But sometimes I think how nice it was when we had the islands all to ourselves."

Post-Mandate
World War II in Europe
1936-1941

In 1936, the Japanese government formally withdrew from the League of Nations, but it continued to file regular reports on the state of the Mandated Islands with the League of Nations.

At that time about 1% of the population in the Northern Mariana Islands was actually indigenous. As a result, the needs of the Japanese people and the interests of the Japanese government increasingly took precedence over those of the Carolinians and Chamorros. The rights these people once enjoyed, such as land ownership and religious freedom, were gradually removed. Islanders were shuffled about and whole villages moved if such action benefited the needs of the Japanese government.

Building an Air-Raid Shelter

Japanese Expansion
Land Acquisitions: 1936–1941

Events Around the World
1936-1941

Europe

1936– Spanish Civil War
    Italians capture Ethiopia

1937– Spanish Civil war continues
    Riots in France
    3,000 Ethiopians killed by Italians

1938– Spanish Civil war continues
    Germans deport thousands of Jews
    Night of Crystal—riots against Jews in Germany

1939– Earthquake in Turkey; 10,000 die
    130,000 Spanish refugees enter France
    Thousands of Jews forced to leave Germany, Hungary, and Czechoslovakia
    16,000 children evacuated from France
    Germans and Soviets invade Poland
    World War II begins
    Soviets invade Finland
    Italians invade Albania

1940– Finland surrenders to Germany
    Germans occupy Denmark & Norway
    German blitzkrieg: Germans invade & capture Brussels, Belgium, Netherlands & France
    Germans bomb Great Britain (The Blitz)
    Italians invade Egypt & Greece
    Allies battle Axis forces in N. Africa

1941– Riots in Rumania; thousands die
    Germans bomb Iceland
    Germans invade Yugoslavia
    Allies drive Axis forces from Ethopia
    Germans invade the Soviet Union

Asia

1936– Japan withdraws from League of Nations

1937– Typhoon kills 300 in Hong Kong
    Japanese capture Peking, China
    Japanese capture Nanking, China; Rape of Nanking
    Japanese invade Shanghai, China
    Panay incident—Japanese sink U.S.S. Panay

1938– Yellow River Dike burst; 15,000 die (China)
    Japanese bomb Chun King, China
    Chinese bomb Japan
    Japanese kill 10,000 near Hankai, China
    Chinese kill 40,000 Japanese near Taierchwan, China
    Japanese use poison gas in China

1939– Japanese occupy French-owned Hainan & Spratly Islands
    Japanese land 60,000 troops in Shanghai

1940– Japanese invade Indochina
    British leave Shanghai, leaving the Japanese in total control
    Australians help defend Singapore

1941– Japanese invade Cambodia and Thailand
    Chinese troops repel Japanese at ChangLa

North America (USA)

1936– Dust Bowl continues

1937– Widespread labor strikes
    Heat wave kills 109
    Gas explosion kills 500 (Texas)
    Hindenburg catches fire, 35 die
    Congressional Report: 1/2 of the nation is ill-housed, ill-clothed and ill-nourished
    Southern states declared to have inadequate living standards

1938– Widespread labor strikes
    Eight million reported jobless
    Flood leaves 20,000 homeless (Calif.)
    5,500 hungry people mob a Republican function (Penn.)

1939– Flash floods kill 100 in New York
    U.S. increases its Defense budget

1940– Congress passes several war preparatory measures including a peacetime draft
    U.S. trades destroyers for bases

1941– Labor strikes across America
    U.S. sends war planes to the Pacific
    U.S. troops land in Iceland
    U.S. supplies war planes to the Soviet Union

EUROPE

ASIA

Northern Mariana Islands
1936-1941
Continued economic prosperity
Military construction begins

North America

"Mom, I want to travel and see the world ..."
"I *still* think you might want to wait a while first ..."

Mandate Revisited

"I've been reviewing the Mandate documents. We were supposed to prepare the indigenous people to become free and self-governing. How were we supposed to have done that anyway?"

"Well, I suppose keeping the natives healthy would have been important ..."

HOSPITAL

"I'd like to see a doctor ..."
"Have a seat."
"Do you know how long I'll have to wait?"
"Quite a while. There's a lot of Okinawans to be treated, too. Maybe you should come in early tomorrow. You would have a better chance of seeing a doctor sooner."

"And we should have helped the natives develop a viable economy so they would become self-sufficient..."

"I'm pleased to announce that in 1935 we exported about 2.5 million yen worth of phosphate, 2 million yen of copra, and 18 million yen of sugar. The Mandated Islands sure have been profitable."

MANDATE EXPORTS
Million Yen

"How much of that income has gone to the natives?"

"This income was derived from Japanese-owned businesses on Japanese-owned land. Why would any of the profits go to the natives?"

"And of course, we would have needed to educate the natives so they would know how to lead and govern."

"Now remember, class, always be diligent, honest, obedient and mindful of your obligations."

"Sensei, how come Japanese students go to school for 8 years and we only go to school for 3?"

"Japanese students need more education because they're training to be leaders and administrators. You only need to learn how to serve and obey.

KOGAKKO

"I guess it's a good thing we're keeping the Mandated Islands. They're definitely not yet ready to be self-governing."

Spying Revisited

Historical records seem to indicate that the Japanese made no effort to construct fortifications within the mandated area until 1939—but the Americans didn't know that...

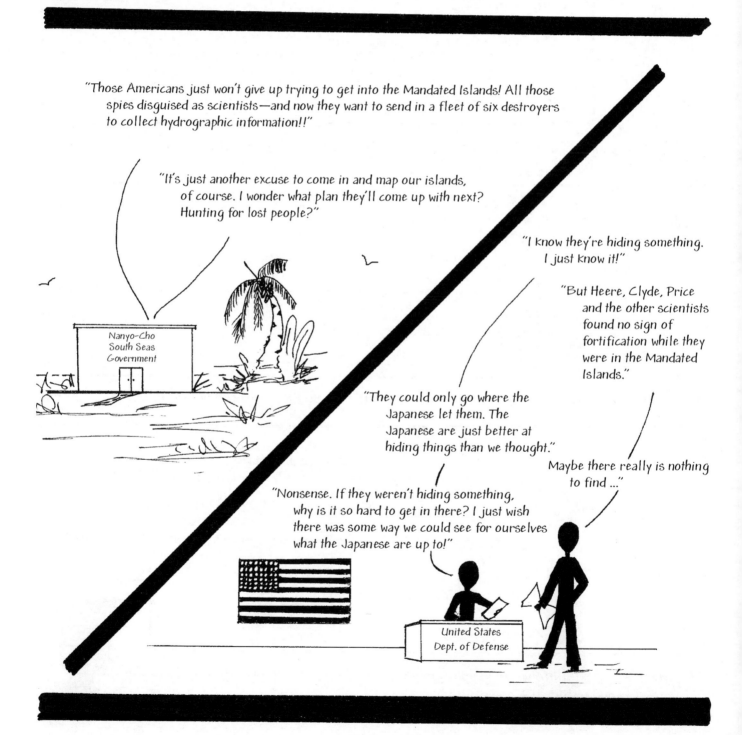

"Those Americans just won't give up trying to get into the Mandated Islands! All those spies disguised as scientists—and now they want to send in a fleet of six destroyers to collect hydrographic information!!"

"It's just another excuse to come in and map our islands, of course. I wonder what plan they'll come up with next? Hunting for lost people?"

Nanyo-Cho
South Seas
Government

"I know they're hiding something. I just know it!"

"But Heere, Clyde, Price and the other scientists found no sign of fortification while they were in the Mandated Islands."

"They could only go where the Japanese let them. The Japanese are just better at hiding things than we thought."

Maybe there really is nothing to find ..."

"Nonsense. If they weren't hiding something, why is it so hard to get in there? I just wish there was some way we could see for ourselves what the Japanese are up to!"

United States
Dept. of Defense

Amelia Earhart

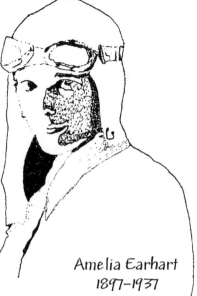

Amelia Earhart was a famous American pilot. She was the first woman to fly solo across the Atlantic Ocean. In May, 1937, Amelia Earhart and her navigator Fred Noonan left Los Angeles, California, and flew East in an attempt to fly around the world. On July 2, 1937, her plane left New Guinea and headed towards Howland Island in the Pacific Ocean. It never arrived. The plane's disappearance sparked a massive sea and air search (9 naval ships and 66 aircraft) by the United States government but no trace was ever found.

Amelia Earhart
1897-1937

The fate of Amelia Earhart and her navigator has been hotly debated ever since. Were they truly lost at sea? Did Amelia Earhart languish and eventually die in a jail on Saipan? Or did something else happen?

"Mama, I think I hear a plane outside..."

"Nonsense, dear. Why would any plane be way out here?"

The Hunt for Amelia

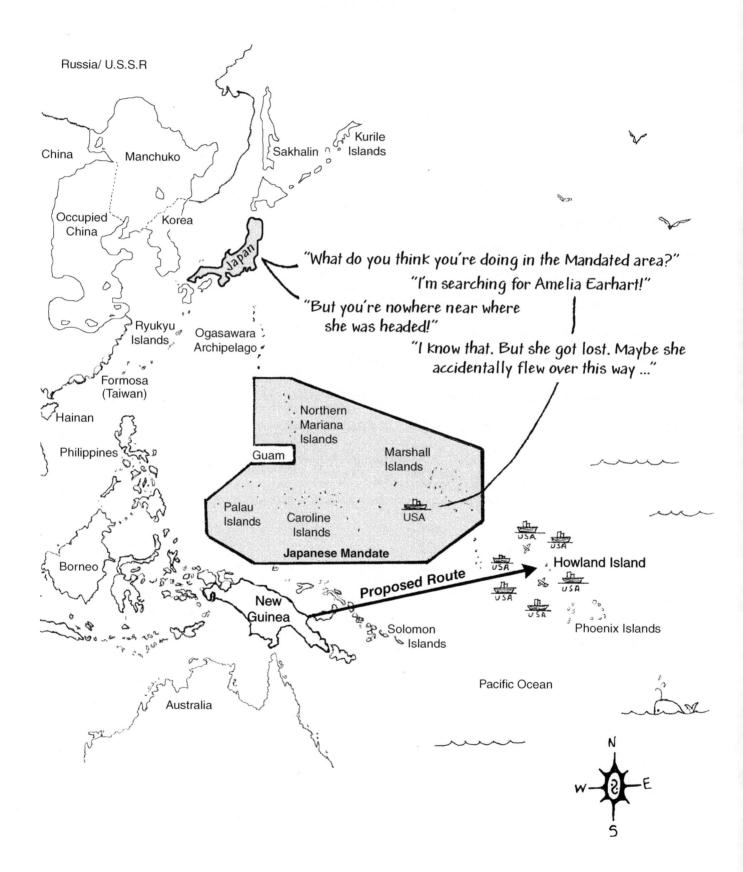

Meanwhile...

As the Japanese government increased its military preparations in the Mandated Islands, the lives of the native population became more difficult.

"I've been looking all over for you! What are you doing way out here?"

"Hiding from the Japanese."

"Whatever for?"

"I heard they're looking for some more people for their heavy construction crew ..."

"Is there room here for me, too?"

The Military Manpower Mobilization Law of 1939 enabled the Japanese government to conscript labor throughout its Empire.

Micronesians, including Chamorros and Carolinians, were pressed into service. They were moved from island to island as needed to work for the Japanese.

The Japanese planned a major military base for Tinian. Twelve hundred Japanese convicts were brought to Tinian at the end of 1939 to construct the airfields. The indigenous inhabitants on Tinian were moved to Saipan and Rota.

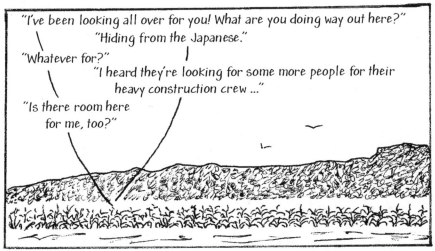

"I just heard they're bringing in convicts to build an airfield here!"

"Convicts! I mean I'm glad it's not us building but convicts! Is that safe?"

"Of course it is. They'll be here and we'll be on Rota."

"Rota? But we live on Tinian!"

"Not any more. We've been ordered to move to Rota immediately."

"Well, I've got to get home. There's Mass to attend tomorrow morning."

"Mass? You don't have to attend that."

"I know. But I have to attend the military drill afterwards."

"So?"

"So I don't figure they're teaching us all those military moves for nothing. One of these days the Japanese may decide to send us all off to war in China or someplace. I figure I'm gonna need all the help I can get."

The Japanese ordered compulsory military drills daily at 5:00 AM. Public celebration of Mass was moved to 4:00 AM.

Tripartite Pact

On September 27, 1940, the Japanese government signed a Tripartite Pact allying itself with Germany and Italy becoming one of the Axis powers.

"Tell me again why we are signing this agreement."

"Well, the interests of Japan and those of Germany are very similar. We both oppose the spread of communism and are engaged in military expansion. Also, we both believe in racial supremacy."

"But the Germans think the Master Race is something called Aryans while we know the superior race is Japanese."

"A minor technicality."

Meanwhile...

In 1941, the Japanese navy formed a defense force in Saipan and brought in about 500 men. Chamorros and Carolinians living in villages on Saipan were forced to move out – their vacated homes were used as housing for the newly arrived men.

After the islanders were forced to move out of the villages and towns, public celebration of Mass stopped. The priest went from farm to farm to perform needed religious services.

Japan invaded China in 1937. As the war with China continued, food shortages developed. Chamorros and Carolinians were not permitted to shop in stores.

World War II
in the Pacific
1941-1944

Japan bombed Pearl Harbor, Hawaii, on December 7, 1941, causing America to declare war on Japan. The increased Japanese military presence in the Northern Mariana Islands due to wartime preparation created shortages. Housing, food and supplies were all reserved for military use. The civilian population was drafted to work on military construction projects and food production.

Japanese treatment of the Chamorros and Carolinians, always strict, became very harsh.

By 1944, food shortages were acute throughout the Northern Mariana Islands due to American blockades. When the Americans bombed and invaded the islands, everyone scrambled to find safe shelter. Hunger and thirst, combined with bombs, bullets and dead bodies, made a most horrific experience.

Japanese Air-Raid Shelter

War Begins

"We've been studying World War II in the Pacific, Grandfather. Do you remember when it began?"

"I remember it well. It was early Monday morning on December 8, after Military Drill. I heard a whole bunch of planes take off and wondered why ... Later I learned that the planes had gone to bomb Guam and that the Japanese had already bombed Pearl Harbor."

"Grandpa, you're funnin' me! The War didn't start on a Monday. It was Sunday, December 7!"

"Not for us. The Japanese bombed Pearl Harbor early Monday morning. And on the very same day they attacked the Philippines, Wake Island, Malaya, Siam, Shanghai, Hong Kong, Wake and Howland Island."

"But the history books say it happened on December 7."

"You're forgetting the International Date Line. Hawaii is on the other side of the Date Line. It may have been December 7 for them, but it was most definitely December 8 for us on Saipan."

"You mean the Japanese ordered that every place designated be attacked on the same day but to do that, some of the planes flying east were flying into the past?"

"Something like that."

"Weird."

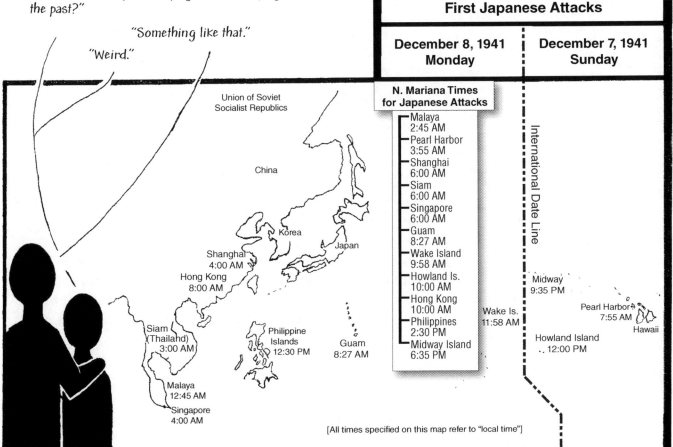

First Japanese Attacks

December 8, 1941 Monday	December 7, 1941 Sunday

N. Mariana Times for Japanese Attacks

- Malaya 2:45 AM
- Pearl Harbor 3:55 AM
- Shanghai 6:00 AM
- Siam 6:00 AM
- Singapore 6:00 AM
- Guam 8:27 AM
- Wake Island 9:58 AM
- Howland Is. 10:00 AM
- Hong Kong 10:00 AM
- Philippines 2:30 PM
- Midway Island 6:35 PM

International Date Line

Union of Soviet Socialist Republics

China

Korea

Japan

Shanghai 4:00 AM

Hong Kong 8:00 AM

Siam (Thailand) 3:00 AM

Philippine Islands 12:30 PM

Guam 8:27 AM

Malaya 12:45 AM

Singapore 4:00 AM

Wake Is. 11:58 AM

Midway 9:35 PM

Pearl Harbor 7:55 AM

Hawaii

Howland Island 12:00 PM

[All times specified on this map refer to "local time"]

Monday, December 8, 1941

After Pearl Harbor had been bombed, the Japanese continued with their plans to attack, invade and capture other American- and British-held lands.

"We want you to come to Guam with us as an interpreter."

"I don't know if I want to be an interpreter ..."

"I can't imagine why you would turn down a chance to serve your Emperor and country. Should you refuse this position, I will have you taken outside and shot as an American spy."

"I guess I'm going to be an interpreter."

"Good decision."

Government Office
Northern Mariana Islands

"Juan! Francesco! Marko! What are you doing here?"

"We overheard the Japanese talking—they plan to invade tomorrow! We had to warn you ..."

"Thanks."

On Monday, December 8, about two dozen men arrived by canoe on Guam from Rota. With them were three men from Saipan who had been told to act as interpreters for the Japanese. The three men from Saipan reported that the Japanese planned to land "tomorrow." They specified the landing location and gave general attack plans ...

The information was greeted with suspicion. Saipanese Charmorros were under Japanese control. Was this a Japanese trick?

The landing site information proved correct, though the actual landing date was Wednesday, December 10.

December 9, 1941
Saipan

"Yesterday, December 7, 1941, a date which will live in infamy—the United States of America was suddenly and deliberately attacked by naval and air forces of the Empire of Japan ..."

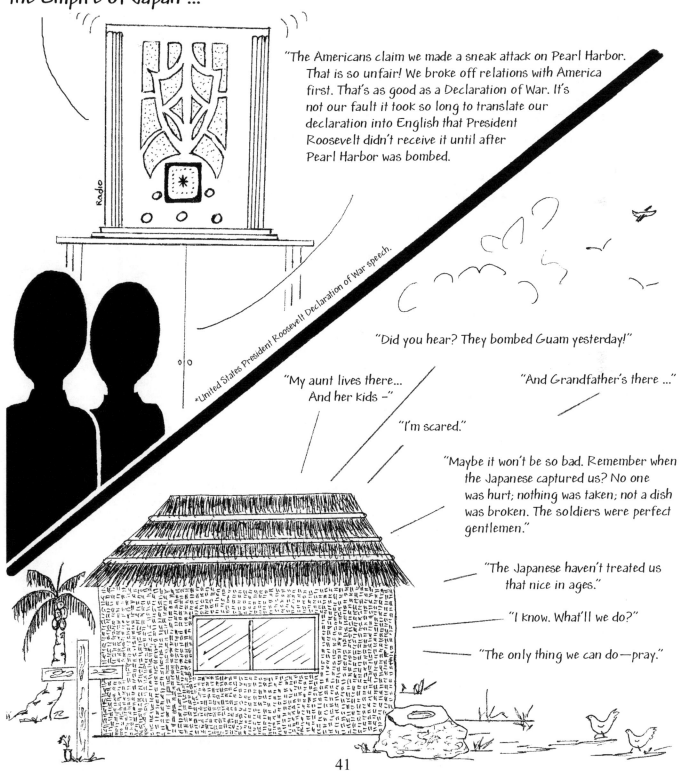

*United States President Roosevelt Declaration of War speech.

"The Americans claim we made a sneak attack on Pearl Harbor. That is so unfair! We broke off relations with America first. That's as good as a Declaration of War. It's not our fault it took so long to translate our declaration into English that President Roosevelt didn't receive it until after Pearl Harbor was bombed.

"Did you hear? They bombed Guam yesterday!"

"My aunt lives there... And her kids –"

"And Grandfather's there ..."

"I'm scared."

"Maybe it won't be so bad. Remember when the Japanese captured us? No one was hurt; nothing was taken; not a dish was broken. The soldiers were perfect gentlemen."

"The Japanese haven't treated us that nice in ages."

"I know. What'll we do?"

"The only thing we can do—pray."

Guam—1941

Guam is the largest island in the Mariana Islands chain. It became a United States territory in 1898. By 1940, Guam had a population of 22,290 people (20,177 Chamorros and 2,113 non-Chamorros). It was defended by 30 U.S. officers and a force of about 500 marines, navy and insular force guards.

On December 10, 1941, approximately 5,000 Japanese military forces landed on the shores of Guam and made their way inland. Vastly outnumbered, Governor George McMillin surrendered at 6:00 AM, but skirmishes continued throughout the island until news of the surrender spread.

The Japanese lost about 10 men. The Americans lost 17. Forty to fifty Chamorro men, women and children died as well. Chamorros were not considered U.S. citizens at the time.

The capture of Guam by the Japanese politically reunited all the Mariana Islands for the first time in 43 years. It was a less than joyful reunion.

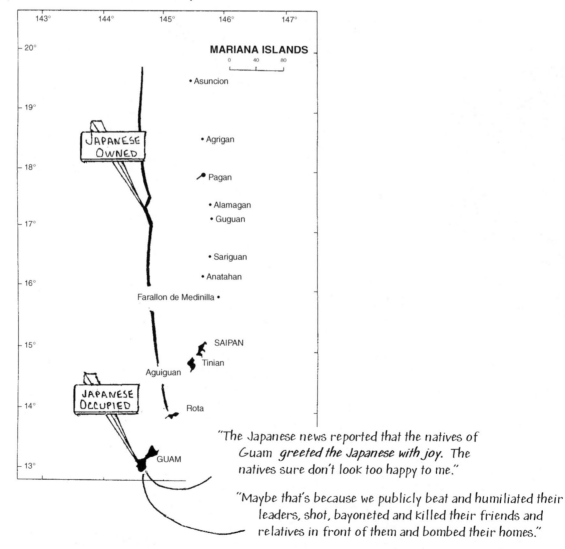

MARIANA ISLANDS

• Asuncion

JAPANESE OWNED

• Agrigan

🖉 Pagan

• Alamagan
• Guguan

• Sariguan

• Anatahan

Farallon de Medinilla •

SAIPAN

Tinian

Aguiguan

JAPANESE OCCUPIED

Rota

GUAM

"The Japanese news reported that the natives of Guam greeted the Japanese with joy. The natives sure don't look too happy to me."

"Maybe that's because we publicly beat and humiliated their leaders, shot, bayoneted and killed their friends and relatives in front of them and bombed their homes."

Japanese Occupation in Guam

Few Japanese spoke either English or Chamorro. Saipanese interpreters were used to convey orders on Guam.

"That's it for interpreting. Why don't you take the rest of the day off and visit with your relatives."

"I'd like to, but...uh...well my aunt and uncle died when a bomb hit their home on December 8. Another aunt was pregnant, but she lost the baby when she was wounded during the invasion. My nephew was bayoneted. Four of my cousins had to give up their homes to the soldiers and my grandmother was beaten because she didn't bow properly ... Frankly, sir, my relatives aren't talking to me right now."

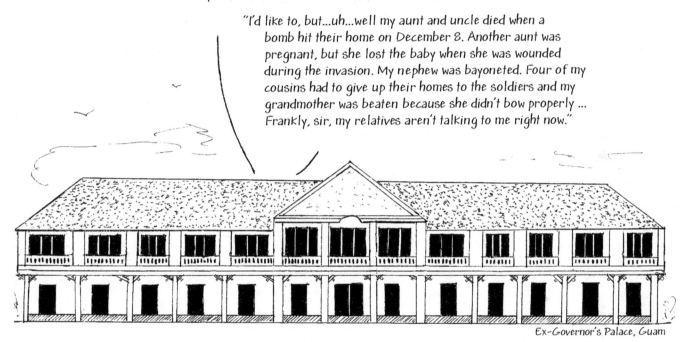

Ex-Governor's Palace, Guam

The Japanese treated the civilians on Guam much as they did the residents of the Northern Mariana Islands.

- They required proper respect for Japanese authority and customs.

- Guamanian children were required to attend school to learn the Japanese language.

- Food supplies were rationed.

- Failure to follow orders or show proper respect was met with swift, often violent, consequences.

In addition, anyone suspected of aiding American resisters was beaten, tortured and/or killed. Execution methods included bayoneting, firing squad (or just shot) and beheading.

Meanwhile ...

On December 11, 1941, Adolph Hitler, Dictator of Germany, declared war on the United States. Rather than attempt to fight a two-front war (against both Japan and Germany at the same time), the United States government chose to send the majority of its troops to Great Britain and assist the Allies in defeating Germany. A naval force remained in the Pacific Ocean. Its primary purpose was to prevent the Japanese from advancing further east.

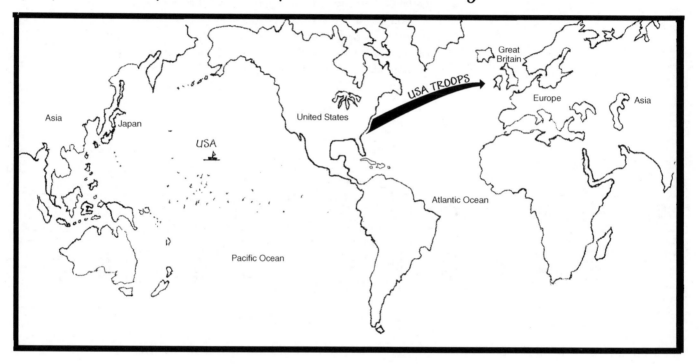

"But I don't understand—Why is the United States sending troops to Europe?"

"Because Germany declared war on the United States."

"But Japan attacked the United States, and the United States declared war on Japan ... Shouldn't it be fighting Japan?"

"Maybe, but then the United States would have to fight Japan alone. If the United States joins the Allies to defeat Germany, then the Allies will assist the United States in defeating Japan. It's always a good idea to have help when fighting a war..."

"So—it was a good thing for the United States that Germany declared war on it?"

"I guess so."

Life for the residents in the Northern Mariana Islands remained much the same as it had before the bombing of Pearl Harbor.

Racial discrimination continued with jobs limited to specific ethnic groups.

The Japanese continued to conscript civilian workers to help on military projects as needed.

Food shortages continued. Food production through farming and fishing was increased. The surplus food was reserved for the military. Sometimes the military paid for the food. Sometimes it didn't.

In an effort to prevent further Japanese westward expansion, the American Air and Naval forces met Japanese Air and Naval forces in combat near Midway Island on June 4, 1942. Japanese losses included four carriers, one heavy cruiser and over 300 planes. American losses included one carrier, one destroyer and about 150 planes.

The Battle of Midway is considered the turning point of the War in the Pacific. After this battle, the Japanese no longer advanced west to capture more land, but instead turned its attention to strengthening existing defenses in an attempt to keep the lands it had already acquired.

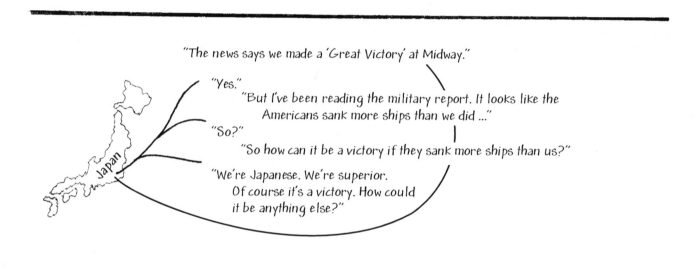

The Japanese government started evacuating Japanese civilians from the Mariana Islands in 1943. Approximately 43,000 Japanese civilians and 4,000 Chamorros and Carolinians lived in the Mariana Islands at that time.

46

In 1943, the Axis troops in Northern Africa surrendered to the Allies. The same year the Allies moved into Sicily and entered Naples, Italy. With the invasion of Europe well under way, the Allies turned more attention towards the defeat of Japan. The American Military developed the strategy of bypassing some Japanese-held islands while attacking others of strategic importance.

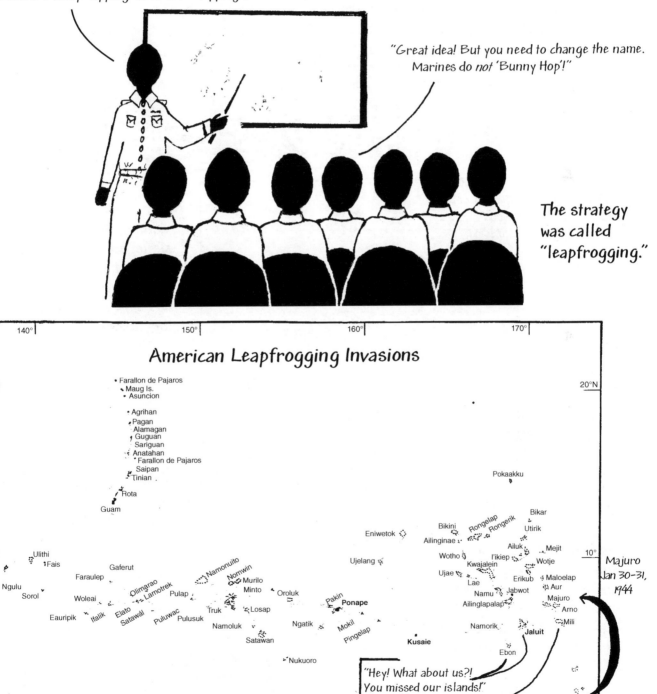

"... and by skipping these islands over here we save lives and reach our objective sooner. I call it 'Bunny Hopping' as we'll be hopping from island to island."

"Great idea! But you need to change the name. Marines do *not* 'Bunny Hop'!"

The strategy was called "leapfrogging."

American Leapfrogging Invasions

Majuro Jan 30-31, 1944

"Hey! What about us?! You missed our islands!"

"Yeah! When do we get to fight?!!"

Tarawa Nov 20-23, 1943

While the fighting continued in Europe, the American Military steadily leapfrogged its way towards the Mariana Islands.

On February 23, 1944, American planes flew over the Mariana Islands taking photos and dropping bombs—168 Japanese aircraft were destroyed.

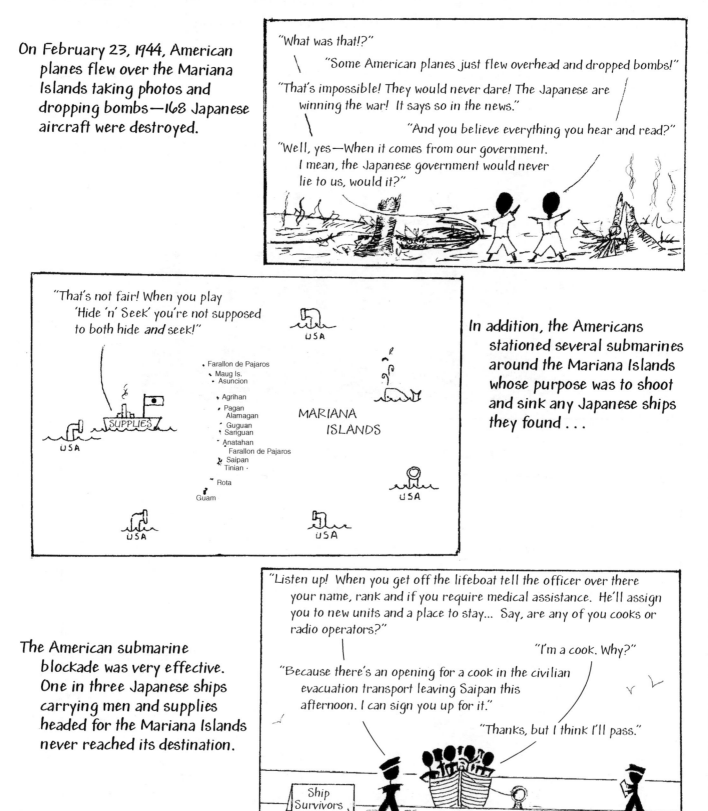

"What was that!?"

"Some American planes just flew overhead and dropped bombs!"

"That's impossible! They would never dare! The Japanese are winning the war! It says so in the news."

"And you believe everything you hear and read?"

"Well, yes—When it comes from our government. I mean, the Japanese government would never lie to us, would it?"

"That's not fair! When you play 'Hide 'n' Seek' you're not supposed to both hide and seek!"

USA

- Farallon de Pajaros
- Maug Is.
- Asuncion
- Agrihan
- Pagan
- Alamagan
- Guguan
- Sariguan
- Anatahan
- Farallon de Pajaros
- Saipan
- Tinian
- Rota
- Guam

MARIANA ISLANDS

SUPPLIES

USA

USA

USA

USA

In addition, the Americans stationed several submarines around the Mariana Islands whose purpose was to shoot and sink any Japanese ships they found . . .

The American submarine blockade was very effective. One in three Japanese ships carrying men and supplies headed for the Mariana Islands never reached its destination.

"Listen up! When you get off the lifeboat tell the officer over there your name, rank and if you require medical assistance. He'll assign you to new units and a place to stay... Say, are any of you cooks or radio operators?"

"I'm a cook. Why?"

"Because there's an opening for a cook in the civilian evacuation transport leaving Saipan this afternoon. I can sign you up for it."

"Thanks, but I think I'll pass."

Ship Survivors →

The Americans decided to invade the Mariana Islands in June, 1944.
By this time ...

... approximately 27,000 Japanese civilians had been evacuated from Saipan.

Over 29,000 Japanese soldiers and sailors were stationed on Saipan preparing its defenses...

Almost 30,000 civilians (roughly 25,000 Japanese, 2,300 Chamorro, 1,300 Korean, and almost 900 Carolinians) remained to face the invasion.

General Yoshitsugo Saito commanded the Japanese military on Saipan. Civilians were ordered to evacuate prime military target areas and build their own shelters.

Miles of tunnels had been dug while numerous bunkers, pill boxes, walls and bomb shelters had been built at strategic locations throughout the Mariana Islands.

Shortages in food, medicine and other supplies intensified due to the blockade.

Anatahan

On June 1, 1944, four days before the Allies entered Rome, Italy, three Japanese transports leaving Saipan were sunk by the Americans. Thirty survivors—29 men and 1 woman—made it to the island of Anatahan. With Japanese attention on preparing defenses for Saipan, the survivors were never rescued by the Japanese ...

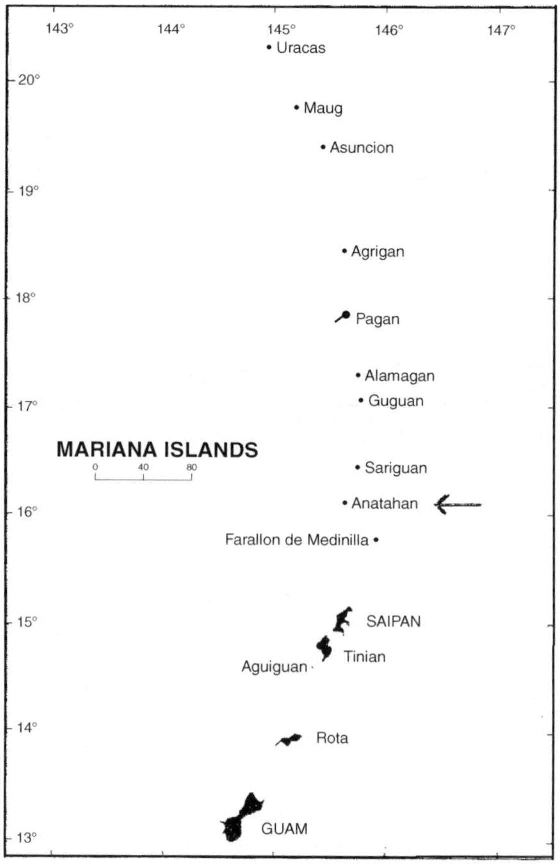

"Hello—are you from the ship too?"

"Yes, miss."

"Are there more survivors?"

"Yes, about 30 of us."

"Oh, good. I wouldn't want to be stranded here all alone ..."

"You certainly won't be alone. Of course, you are the only woman."

MARIANA ISLANDS

- Uracas
- Maug
- Asuncion
- Agrigan
- Pagan
- Alamagan
- Guguan
- Sariguan
- Anatahan ←
- Farallon de Medinilla
- SAIPAN
- Tinian
- Aguiguan
- Rota
- GUAM

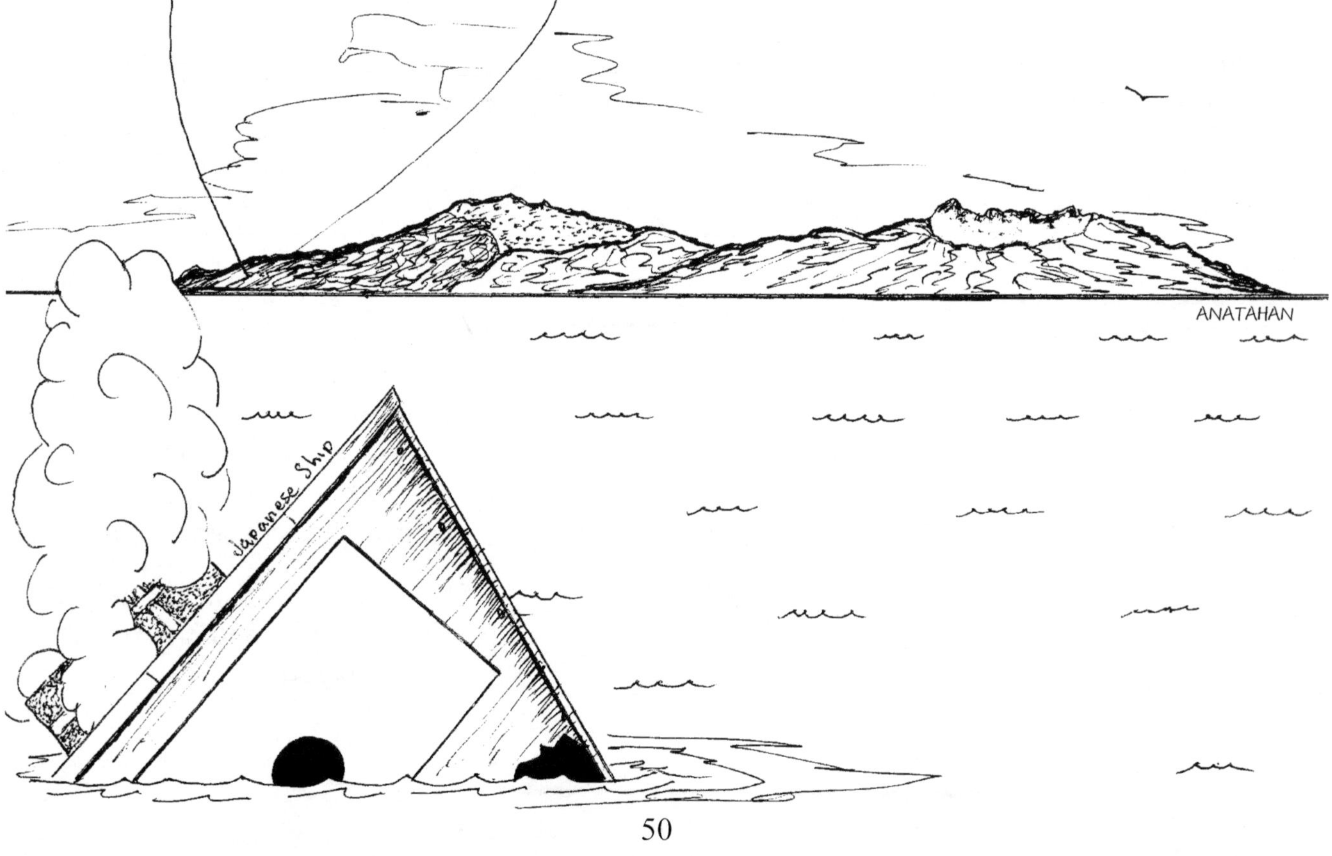

0 40 80

143° 144° 145° 146° 147°
20° 19° 18° 17° 16° 15° 14° 13°

ANATAHAN

Japanese Ship

The War Comes to Saipan

At 8:15 AM on June 15, 1944, nine days after the Allied invasion of Normandy, France, over 8,000 American troops stormed the beaches of Saipan. They were met with heavy Japanese artillery fire. The Americans suffered over 2,000 casualties by the end of the day. The Japanese counterattacked during the night in an effort to drive the Americans from the beach. The Americans fired star shells into the air turning night into day so they could see to fight. Over 700 Japanese soldiers lay dead the next morning. The Americans retained control of the beach and the fighting continued.

BOOM! BOOM!

"Hurry! Get the kids together and grab all our food. We've got to get to the cave NOW!"

"Why? Are the Japanese coming?"

"Worse! The Americans!"

The Chamorros, Carolinians and other civilians sought shelter wherever they could. Most hid in caves. There were many caves scattered throughout Saipan.

The American invasion caused much suffering among the civilians on Saipan. They had little or no food or water. Bombs burst overhead and bullets flew everywhere all causing injury and death.

"I'm hungry, Mom."

"Me, too!"

"I know. Be patient. Your dad has gone out to look for some food. He should be back soon."

"But it's dark out! How will he see to find anything?"

PSSST! PSSST Boom!

"I don't think that will be a problem ..."

Boom!

"That's it? Just a wire fence. No shelter, toilets, anything?"

"At least they gave us some food and water, and we don't have to worry about people shooting at us.

BAM!! BAM!!

"Rather, we don't have to worry about the Americans shooting at us."

By June 16, the Americans had over 1,000 refugees seeking to escape the fighting. Separated by race, the refugees were placed in stockades built on the beach. They had no shelter and had to huddle on the sand, while the battle raged on around them.

The Fighting Continues

"I've received word that neither reinforcements nor air support will be arriving..."

"That doesn't make sense. I heard on the radio that we just won a great victory over the Americans in the Philippine Sea. Surely our forces are now free to come to our aid ..."

"Unfortunately, I think the news may have exaggerated our 'victory' in the Philippine Sea a bit ..."

On June 19, 1944, American forces met Japanese forces in combat in the Philippine Sea west of the Mariana Islands.

By the end of the day, the Americans had lost 130 planes, while the Japanese lost 3 carriers, 2 fleet tankers and 476 planes.

As a result of the Battle of the Philippine Sea, the Japanese were unable to provide air support or reinforcements to their troops on Saipan. This guaranteed the eventual success of the Americans in their efforts to capture Saipan.

The Japanese soldiers used guerrilla warfare against their American enemies. They hid in trees, ditches, tunnels, caves—wherever they could. They killed, or tried to kill, every American soldier possible.

"Hide 'n' Seek was a lot more fun when those hiding didn't shoot back."

"All the caves are full! Where can I go that's safe?"

"I just left a cave over that way. They've space and they'll probably let you in if you promise to be quiet."

"Thanks. Wait a minute. Why did you leave?"

"I was afraid my baby would start crying. The soldiers in the cave were killing any baby that wouldn't keep quiet."

Chamorros, Carolinians and Japanese all took refuge in caves to avoid the bombs, bullets and advancing Americans.

Hunger, thirst, exhaustion and a sense of impending doom mingled with the fear of being captured by the "dreaded" Americans.

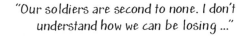

"Our soldiers are second to none. I don't understand how we can be losing ..."

Despite fierce opposition, the Americans continued to push forward gaining more land daily on Saipan.

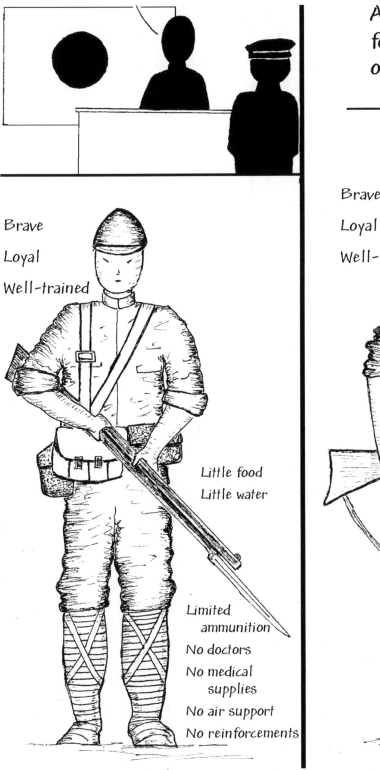

Brave

Loyal

Well-trained

Little food
Little water

Limited ammunition

No doctors

No medical supplies

No air support

No reinforcements

Japanese Soldier

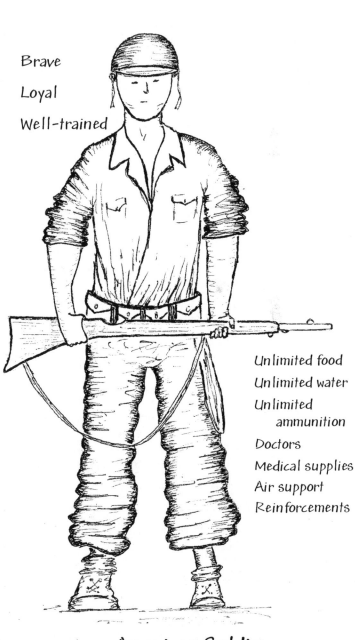

Brave

Loyal

Well-trained

Unlimited food
Unlimited water
Unlimited ammunition
Doctors
Medical supplies
Air support
Reinforcements

American Soldier

On June 20, the Americans moved the refugees to a more permanent facility later named Camp Susupe.

The Americans recruited refugees to help locate occupied caves and convince the inhabitants to leave.

Taught that Americans were barbaric devils, the Japanese civilians were reluctant to believe otherwise.

"... get a stick, tie a white cloth to it and walk out with your hands up. I swear, they won't hurt you. They'll give you some food, water and medicine, if you need it."

"I don't believe you! The Americans are going to torture and eat us if we come out."

"And you know this because?"

"Because our teachers said it; the newspaper says it; the radio says it; our government says it!"

"Is that the same government that said Americans were cowards and promised they would never invade Saipan?"

"?! —Good point. Let's find a white rag ..."

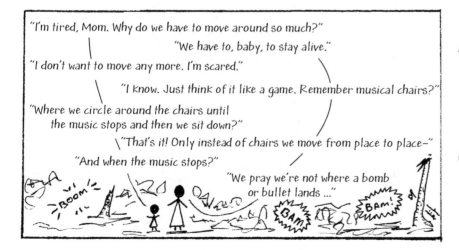

"I'm tired, Mom. Why do we have to move around so much?"

"We have to, baby, to stay alive."

"I don't want to move any more. I'm scared."

"I know. Just think of it like a game. Remember musical chairs?"

"Where we circle around the chairs until the music stops and then we sit down?"

"That's it! Only instead of chairs we move from place to place—"

"And when the music stops?"

"We pray we're not where a bomb or bullet lands ..."

Civilians behind Japanese lines struggled to stay alive. Some were fortunate to find shelter safe enough to remain in one place throughout the fighting.

Others had to shift from hiding place to hiding place to stay alive.

54

Bushido

Japanese culture is steeped in the concept of Bushido—the willingness to accept death without a whimper and to commit suicide because doing so is advancing a lofty cause. The Japanese military added to this basic belief the idea that there could be no surrender, no defeat—the solider achieved victory or he died. All of this combined to make a most formidable fighting machine.

"I actually got some soldiers to surrender yesterday."

"Really? Japanese?"

"No. Koreans."

Japanese soldiers did not acknowledge defeat. They kept on fighting even in the face of overwhelming opposition.

Of the over 30,000 Japanese military on Saipan, only 2,100 were taken prisoner. Those who were captured expressed surprise at the humane treatment they received.

Japanese soldiers were known to kill their own wounded and to commit suicide rather than risk the shame and humiliation of capture by the Americans.

"He looks injured—maybe we can convince him to surrender ..."

BOOM!!!

"Too late! That must have been a grenade in his hand."

"Our commander has died most honorably."

"He took the easy way."

"How can you say that? It is most difficult to commit a proper suicide."

"True. But I think it is more difficult to try to stay alive long enough to kill 7 Americans ..."

Last Japanese Command Post, Saipan

Realizing the battle was lost and refusing to surrender, General Saito ordered his soldiers to launch a final Banzai attack. He charged each man to "take seven lives"—a final "blow to the American Devils." General Saito then committed ritual suicide.

Early next morning at 4:00 AM July 7, thousands of Japanese soldiers, some armed only with knives and sharpened sticks, charged the American lines. When the attack ended, 4,311 Japanese soldiers lay dead.

Organized Japanese resistance on Saipan ended after the Banzai attack.

Suicide Cliff

As American forces moved forward, Japanese civilians retreated north seeking shelter from bombs and bullets. Convinced that they would suffer unspeakable horror and death at the hands of the American soldiers, thousands of Japanese civilians chose to end their lives. Some jumped off the cliffs into the ocean. Others clustered around a grenade, which was then exploded. Hundreds of civilian men, women, and children made their way to the top of Mount Marpi and jumped off the cliffs to certain death. Some have estimated over 20,000 civilians committed suicide on Saipan. Today, Mount Marpi is referred to as "Suicide Cliff."

Marpi Point
Mount Marpi
Managaha Island
Mount Tapochau

American Invasion of Saipan
June 15–
July 9, 1944

"Where are you going?"

"To the top of Mount Marpi to jump off."

"Why?"

"Because the American are coming! They will rape the women and eat the babies."

"You really believe that?"

"Of course. Our government says so. Why would our government lie? Besides, I heard that's what our soldiers did in China. The Americans are barbarians. They're bound to be much worse! It's better to die with honor than be captured by Americans. Are you coming?"

"No. We're Catholics. We don't believe in suicide."

"You'll be sorry."

"I hope not."

MOUNT MARPI, SAIPAN

The Fighting Continues ...

"You were ordered to return to the ship ages ago. What took you so long?"

"Sorry, sir, but there were so many bodies in the water, we couldn't go any faster for fear they would jam the propeller."

Hundreds of soldiers and civilians ended their lives in the surf off Marpi Point, Saipan (now referred to as "Bonsai Cliff"). The waters below the Point became so thick with the bodies of men, women, and children that small naval craft were unable to steer a course without running over them.

The leap off Marpi Point did not guarantee certain death. Fifty to sixty Japanese soldiers who survived the leap managed to swim to a reef. Using machine guns, the Japanese fired upon the Americans. They did not stop until they were all killed by the Americans.

Japanese suicide survivors climbed upon other reefs off Saipan as well.

"Look! There are some more survivors. Do you suppose they'll let us capture them or will we have to kill them?"

"Neither—see the one standing? He's beheading the others ..."

"How can we keep the Americans from killing us?"

"Their war is against the Japanese, not us. Tell them we're Chamorros and maybe they'll leave us alone."

"That won't work. They don't speak Chamorro and I don't speak American—do you?"

"There must be something we can do ..."

"Hold your fire, men. I see a cross. There must be natives inside this cave—The Japanese wouldn't use a cross ..."

Prior contact with the Americans on Guam caused the Chamorros and Carolinians to doubt that capture by the Americans would be as bad as the Japanese government claimed.

Staying alive throughout all the gunfire was still difficult ...

At 4:15 PM, July 9, 1944, after 24 days of fighting, Admiral Turner of the American forces announced Saipan was "secured." There were no more major battles on Saipan. An estimated 14,100 Americans were killed, wounded or "missing in action" as a result of the fighting.

While there were no more major battles, there was still "mopping up" to be done—locating and neutralizing the remaining pockets of enemy soldiers still hiding in caves, ravines, and gullies throughout Saipan.

Managahan is a tiny island (250 yards wide, 300 yards long) in Tanapeg Harbor, some 2,500 yards from the shores of Saipan. It held 29 Japanese defenders.

On July 15, 1944, the Americans invaded Managaha. After an hour the island was secured, and 13 Japanese soldiers were captured. The rest lay dead. Only one American soldier was wounded during the operation.

On July 21, 1944, the Americans invaded Guam. The Chamorros of Guam were most pleased with the arrival of the Americans. They had endured 2½ years of martial law under the Japanese and had little love for their Japanese captors, or anyone who had helped them.

War Dogs

On July 21, 1944, the 1st, 2nd, and 3rd Marine Dog Platoons (60 dogs) arrived on Guam. The dogs were trained primarily as messenger or scout dogs. Messenger dogs carried messages, ammunition and/or medicine between two handlers, one near the front and the other behind the lines. Scout dogs were trained to give silent warnings at the approach of any enemy.

The dogs explored caves, pill boxes, dugouts, other structures and fortified positions, alerting their handlers to any occupied areas. The presence of dogs reduced the danger of ambush, boosted morale and enabled patrols to operate more efficiently.

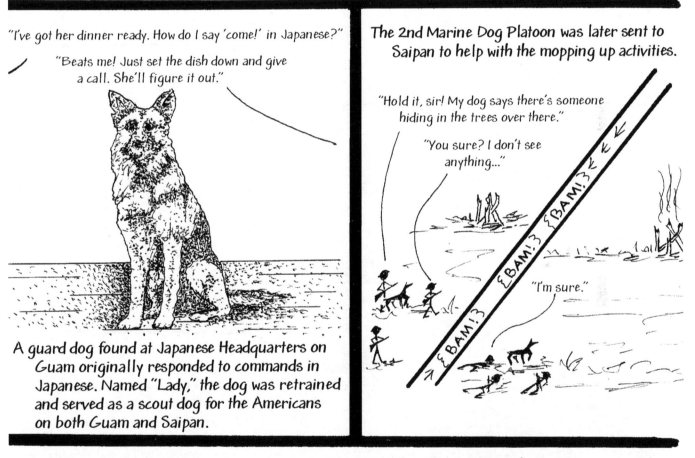

"I've got her dinner ready. How do I say 'come!' in Japanese?"

"Beats me! Just set the dish down and give a call. She'll figure it out."

A guard dog found at Japanese Headquarters on Guam originally responded to commands in Japanese. Named "Lady," the dog was retrained and served as a scout dog for the Americans on both Guam and Saipan.

The 2nd Marine Dog Platoon was later sent to Saipan to help with the mopping up activities.

"Hold it, sir! My dog says there's someone hiding in the trees over there."

"You sure? I don't see anything..."

"I'm sure."

Twenty-four dogs died during the campaign of Guam. They are buried and honored in a special cemetery on the U.S. Naval base at Orote Point, Guam.

"I thought you said we were helping to get ready for Memorial Day. This is a dog cemetery!"

"These dogs died during World War II. They were specially trained to deliver messages, despite bombs exploding all around. They provided advance warning of enemy attack and located enemy snipers hiding in the trees and caves. They saved a whole bunch of lives!"

"You mean they aren't just dogs, they're heroes!"

"Yep!"

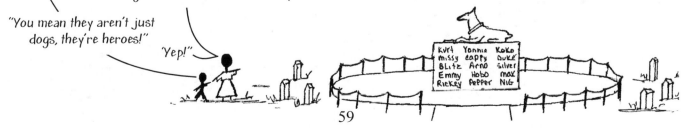

Tinian

At 5:30 AM, July 24, 1944, seven large transport ships arrived off the shore of Tinian Town, Tinian. Marines proceeded to disembark and were met by heavy gunfire ...

This was a fake attack. The actual landing and attack occurred on the same day at 7:20 AM on two tiny beaches (one 60 yards wide; the other 160 yards wide) on the Northwestern side of Tinian. There was little resistance. By the end of the day, the Americans had landed 15,614 marines. Only 77 lives were lost.

Admiral Spruance later wrote, "In my opinion, the Tinian operation was probably the most brilliantly conceived and executed operation in World War II."

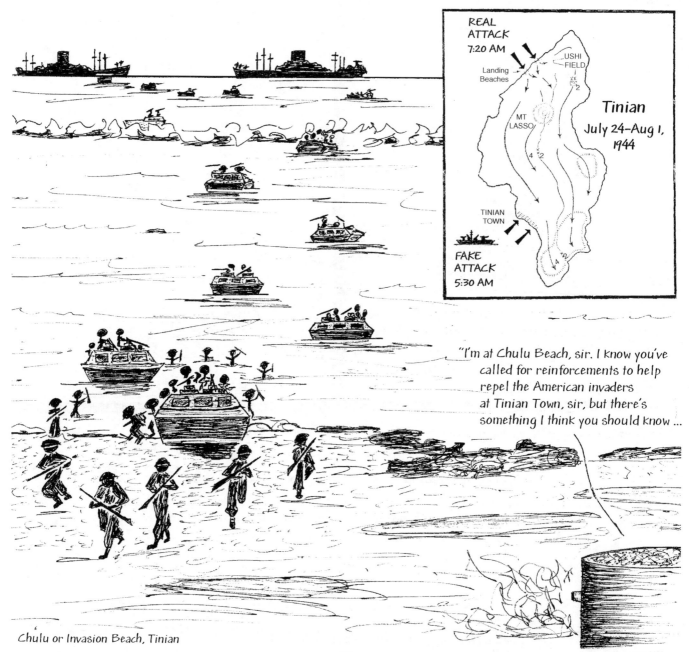

"I'm at Chulu Beach, sir. I know you've called for reinforcements to help repel the American invaders at Tinian Town, sir, but there's something I think you should know ...

Chulu or Invasion Beach, Tinian

Japanese Pillbox

On the night of July 24, the Japanese launched a counter attack on Tinian.

After a night of furious fighting, which included Japanese tanks and American bazookas, the Americans retained control of Tinian shores. In the morning, 1,241 Japanese soldiers lay dead.

A typhoon struck Tinian July 28-29. Despite high winds, rain and heavy swells, the Americans continued to shuttle artillery to firing positions and carry supplies to inland dumps and men on the front lines.

On July 30, the Americans moved into Tinian Town (present day San Jose Village). Constant American shelling had turned the town into rubble.

Napalm

Napalm is the name given to flammable liquids used in warfare, often jellied gasoline. Napalm burns at a specific rate and sticks to any material it touches. Napalm is used in flame throwers. Flame throwers are very effective weapons. The flames can go around corners. In addition, the flames swiftly use up the oxygen in an enclosed room, often suffocating and killing those who survive the flames.

Flame throwers were used by American soldiers on both Saipan and Tinian to silence Japanese gunfire from caves, pill boxes and other forms of fortifications.

The first napalm bombs used in the Pacific were dropped on Tinian. The resulting fires burned the foliage making it easier for American soldiers to see the Japanese and their fortifications.

The Navajo Code Talkers

The Americans recruited over 400 Navajo Indians to help with communication. The Navajos combined their language with code words to make an oral code used over the radio when reporting troop movement and needs.

The Japanese could not translate the Navajo messages so the Americans were assured complete secrecy when sending or receiving messages on the battlefield.

The Navajo Code Talkers were used extensively throughout the Pacific including on Saipan, Tinian and Guam. Their help was invaluable in enabling the Americans to capture the Mariana Islands.

Civilians

Every day 500-600 civilian refugees crossed the American lines. They were placed under the care of the Marine Civil Affairs officers.

The American Red Cross provided immediate relief, but unfortunately many civilian refugees still died from their wounds.

"I heard your sister just died. I'm so sorry."

"Me, too. At least she died here."

"What do you mean?"

"Well, my sister got injured when the bombs exploded, but the rest of my family died at the same time. I don't even know where their bodies are! At least my sister will get a proper burial.."

Over half the refugees were children under the age of 15. Many of the children were orphaned as a result of the fighting.

"Mama?"

"Your mama's not here anymore, sweetie. But I'll be your mama if you wish."

"That's so nice of you to take care of that orphan."

"Well, she gives me purpose and helps me forget my own losses."

"How many have you adopted?"

"Twenty-eight, but who's counting?"

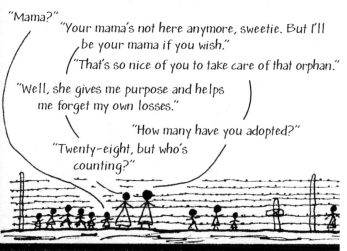

Relief planners intended to use existing structures as relief shelters and/or salvage purposes. It was a challenging task.

"What are you doing out here?"

"Looking for some structures or building materials to use for the civilian refugees."

"Good luck!"

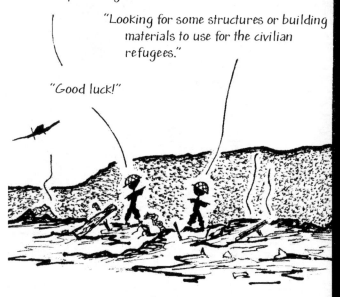

The initial daily diet per civilian was: 8 ounces rice, 4 ounces flour, 2 ounces vegetables, .6 ounces fish, .2 ounces sugar, .2 ounces fats, and .5 ounces salt.

"...there's a mistake in the amount of food you're to give each civilian."

"I knew it! What I've been passing out is barely enough to survive! What should it be?"

"Instead of six ounces of fish, it should be six-tenths of an ounce of fish."

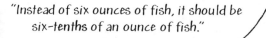

Marine Civil Affairs

August, 1944

On August 1, 1944, 6:55 PM, the Americans declared the Island of Tinian "secured." Of the 9,000 Japanese military defending Tinian, only 252 became prisoners.

On August 15, 1944, the Island of Guam was also declared "secured." All that remained to be done on Saipan, Tinian and Guam was the "mopping up" operations—finding the Japanese still hiding.

This ended the formal fighting in the Mariana Islands, but it did not end World War II or Japanese control in the Northern Mariana Islands. Several Northern Mariana Islands had been "leapfrogged" over. They were bombed periodically but never invaded. No outside food or supplies reached those islands during the rest of the war.

While 15,000 civilians lived behind American stockades on Saipan awaiting the end of the war, about 5,000 Japanese troops and almost 800 Chamorros and Carolinians resided on Rota.

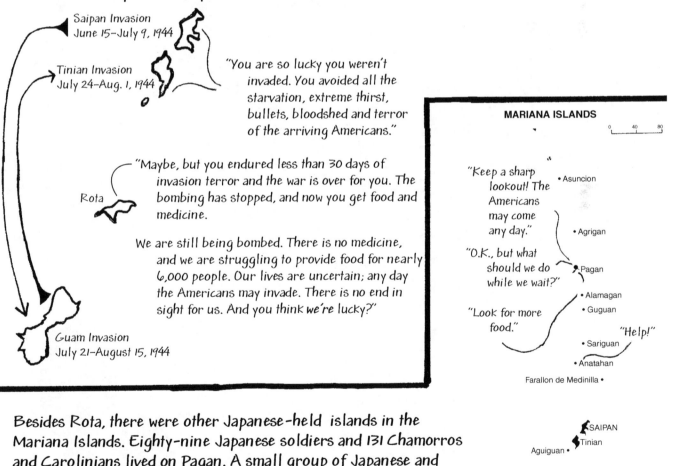

Saipan Invasion
June 15–July 9, 1944

Tinian Invasion
July 24–Aug. 1, 1944

"You are so lucky you weren't invaded. You avoided all the starvation, extreme thirst, bullets, bloodshed and terror of the arriving Americans."

Rota

"Maybe, but you endured less than 30 days of invasion terror and the war is over for you. The bombing has stopped, and now you get food and medicine.

We are still being bombed. There is no medicine, and we are struggling to provide food for nearly 6,000 people. Our lives are uncertain; any day the Americans may invade. There is no end in sight for us. And you think *we're* lucky?"

Guam Invasion
July 21–August 15, 1944

MARIANA ISLANDS

0   40   80

"Keep a sharp lookout! The Americans may come any day."

• Asuncion

• Agrigan

"O.K., but what should we do while we wait?"

Pagan

• Alamagan

• Guguan

"Look for more food."

"Help!"

• Sariguan

• Anatahan

Farallon de Medinilla •

SAIPAN

Tinian

Aguiguan •

Rota

GUAM

Besides Rota, there were other Japanese-held islands in the Mariana Islands. Eighty-nine Japanese soldiers and 131 Chamorros and Carolinians lived on Pagan. A small group of Japanese and Okinawans lived on Aguigun, too. In addition, 29 men and one woman, Japanese castaways, were still on Anathahan awaiting rescue.

The inhabitants of all these Japanese-held islands had to live off the land and sea, making do or doing without, while they waited for the end of the war.

EPILOGUE

And so, this little history ends for now. The Chamorros and Carolinians lived under the authority of the Spanish, the Germans, and the Japanese. How will they fare at the hands of the Americans?

To be continued ...

Acknowledgements

I would like to thank all those people whose ideas and encouragement made this book possible.

While many people were involved in the creation of this book, some especially stand out in my mind. I especially wish to acknowledge the Sisters at the San Jose Church on Tinian. After reading History of the Northern Mariana Islands, Part I, their first words to me were "When is Part II coming?" Their faith in me kept me writing.

Special recognition should go to my sister, Bonnie Battaglia, a reference librarian, who helped with the research. I would also like to thank my parents, both of whom are World War II Veterans. My father Angelo ("Batt") Battaglia was a pilot in the Army Air Force, and at a glance, could tell a Lockheed Electra plane from a Beech; he read every word and studied every picture, keeping me on my toes for artistic and historic accuracy. My mother, Mary Jane (Dean) Battaglia, served in the Navy WAVES as a Link Trainer Operator. While critically reading my work, looking for gaps in the information presented and helping me with vigorous proofreading, she pondered the fate of her former students—Navy and Marine pilots who had been slated for duty in the Pacific.

Finally, I would like to thank my husband, Howard Cole, for his encouragement and support, and my daughter, Amanda, who read my cartoons enthusiastically.

Bibliography

Most of the information for this history comes from the following sources:

Aaseng, Nathan. *Navajo Code Talkers*. New York: Walker Publishing Company, 1992.

Bowers, Neal M. *Problems of Resettlement on Saipan, Tinian, and Rota, Mariana Islands*. N.M.I.: Division of Historic Preservation, June 2001 (second edition). First published in 1950.

Chant, Christopher, ed. *The Marshall Cavendish Illustrated Encyclopedia of World War II, Volume 22*. London: Orbis Publishing Limited, 1972.

Collier's Photographic History of World War II. New York: P.F. Collier & Son Corporation, 1944.

Collins, Brigadier General James L. Jr., ed. *The Marshall Cavendish Illustrated Encyclopedia of World War II, The Pacific War*. London: Orbis Publishing Limited, 1972.

Costello, John. *The Pacific War*. New York: Rawson, Wade Publishers, Inc.,1981.

Crowl, Philip A. *U.S. Army in World War II, The War in the Pacific*. Washington, D.C.: Center of Military History, United States Army, 1960.

Farrell, Don A. *History of the Northern Mariana Islands*. Commonwealth of the Northern Mariana Islands: Public School System, 1991.

———. *Liberation-1944*. Tamuning, Guam: Micronesian Productions, 1984.

———. *Saipan*. Commonwealth of the Northern Mariana Islands: Micronesian Productions, 1993.

———. *Tinian*. Commonwealth of the Northern Mariana Islands: Micronesian Productions, 1992.

———. *The Sacrifice 1919-1943*. Tinian, Commonwealth of the Northern Mariana Islands: Micronesian Productions, 1991.

Hamer, Blythe. *Dogs at War*. London: Carlton Books Ltd., 2001.

Hane, Mikiso. *Japan, A Historical Survey*. New York: Charles Scribner's Sons, 1972.

Heffer, Jean. *The United States and the Pacific, History of a Frontier*. Notre Dame, IN: University of Notre Dame Press, 2002.

Hoffman, Major Carl W. *Saipan: The Beginning of the End*. Nashville, TN: Battery Press, Inc., 1988.